翻译研究论丛

《老子》译话

许渊冲 ◎著

图书在版编目(CIP)数据

《老子》译话 / 许渊冲著. —北京：北京大学出版社，2016.10
（翻译研究论丛）
ISBN 978-7-301-27677-8

Ⅰ. ①老… Ⅱ. ①许… Ⅲ. ①道家 ②《道德经》– 译文 Ⅳ. ① B223.14

中国版本图书馆 CIP 数据核字 (2016) 第 256966 号

书　　　名	《老子》译话 LAOZI YIHUA
著作责任者	许渊冲　著
责任编辑	郝妮娜
标准书号	ISBN 978-7-301-27677-8
出版发行	北京大学出版社
地　　　址	北京市海淀区成府路 205 号　100871
网　　　址	http://www.pup.cn　新浪微博：@北京大学出版社
电子信箱	bdhnn2011@126.com
电　　　话	邮购部 62752015　发行部 62750672　编辑部 62759634
印 刷 者	北京大学印刷厂
经 销 者	新华书店
	650 毫米 ×980 毫米　16 开本　15.25 印张　300 千字 2016 年 10 月第 1 版　2019 年 8 月第 2 次印刷
定　　　价	45.00 元

未经许可，不得以任何方式复制或抄袭本书之部分或全部内容。
版权所有，侵权必究
举报电话：010-62752024　电子信箱：fd@pup.pku.edu.cn
图书如有印装质量问题，请与出版部联系，电话：010-62756370

目 录

第一章	总　论	1
第二章	辩证法	7
第三章	论无为	11
第四章	论道冲	13
第五章	论不仁	15
第六章	论空灵	17
第七章	论无私	20
第八章	论不争	23
第九章	论自满	25
第十章	论魂魄	28
第十一章	论有无	32
第十二章	论声色	35
第十三章	论荣辱	38
第十四章	论道纪	41
第十五章	论识道	44
第十六章	论常道	47
第十七章	论治国	50
第十八章	论正反	52
第十九章	论弃绝	55

第二十章	论独异	58
第二十一章	论物象	61
第二十二章	论曲直	64
第二十三章	论希言	68
第二十四章	论自见	71
第二十五章	论大道	73
第二十六章	论轻重	75
第二十七章	论善行	77
第二十八章	论知守	79
第二十九章	论为之	82
第三十章	论兵强	84
第三十一章	论吉凶	86
第三十二章	论道常	89
第三十三章	论知行	92
第三十四章	论大道	95
第三十五章	论道感	97
第三十六章	论刚柔	99
第三十七章	论无为	102
第三十八章	论　德	104
第三十九章	论得道	109
第四十章	论反复	112
第四十一章	谈闻道	115
第四十二章	正反合	120
第四十三章	柔与刚	123
第四十四章	得与失	126

第四十五章	论大成	129
第四十六章	论知足	132
第四十七章	论天道	135
第四十八章	论损益	137
第四十九章	论常心	140
第五十章	论生死	142
第五十一章	论道德	145
第五十二章	论习常	148
第五十三章	论大道	151
第五十四章	论修道	154
第五十五章	论厚德	157
第五十六章	论玄同	160
第五十七章	治国论	163
第五十八章	论祸福	165
第五十九章	论积德	167
第六十章	论德归	170
第六十一章	论下流	173
第六十二章	善与恶	176
第六十三章	难与易	181
第六十四章	成与败	186
第六十五章	智与愚	189
第六十六章	论不争	192
第六十七章	慈之道	195
第六十八章	智仁勇	198
第六十九章	攻与守	201

第七十章	内与外	204
第七十一章	认识论	207
第七十二章	论不厌	210
第七十三章	论争胜	213
第七十四章	论畏死	215
第七十五章	论生死	218
第七十六章	论强弱	221
第七十七章	论高下	224
第七十八章	论刚柔	227
第七十九章	论德怨	230
第八十章	论小国	233
第八十一章	论信美	235

第一章

总　论

《老子》是中国最早的哲学著作，比西方的希腊哲学约早一二百年，内容深刻，文字精练，影响深远，可以和希腊的柏拉图思想争辉比美，毫不逊色。

《老子》第一章说："道可道，非常道。"第一个"道"就是老子哲学的本体论。"道"字意义丰富，很难译成英文，一般音译为 Tao，"道家"半音译半意译为 Taoist，已经为辞典所接受，但是不好理解，有人直译为 Way（道路），比较具体；有人意译为 Law（道理、规律），比较抽象；有人折中译成 Truth（道理，真理），到底如何译好，要看具体上下文内容来决定，"道可道"中的第二个"道"是动词，是"说道""知道"的意思，说"道"是可以知道的，可以认识的，这是老子哲学的认识论，"道可道"说明老子的认识论不是"不可知论"，而是"可知论"，怎么"可知"呢？老子回答说："非常道。"这就是说："道"是可以知道，可以认识的，但不一定是大家常说的道理。举个例子来说：民主的道理是可以知道的，但不一定是美国人常说的那个民主的道理。美国林肯总统理解的民主,是一个民有,民治,民享的政府(a government of the people, by the people, for the people)。但是到了今天,美国强调的是民治,是民选,而中国强调的是民享,是为人民服务。现在,西方国家认为中国不是民主国家,但中国认为西方民主并不民主,就以民选而论,布什和戈尔竞选美国总统时,布什得票少于戈尔反而当选,难道这是民主吗?中国虽然没有像美国那样进行选举,但人民对"民享"的政府是满意的。所以,到底是美国民治的道理,还是中国民享的道理对呢?看来还是老子说得不错:"道可道,非常道。"民主的道理是可以知道的,但既不是美国人常说的民选民治之道,也不是中国常说的为人民服务之道。这就是老子哲学的认识论。《老子》第一章前六个字就包含了本体论和认识论,多么精炼,多么丰富,多么深刻。这句话国内有几种译文:

  1. The Tao that is utterable is not the eternal Tao. (北京大学出版社)

  2. The Dao that can be told is not the constant Dao. (外文出版社)

  3. The Way can be expressed, but the Way that can be expressed is not the eternal Way. (世界图书出版公司)

  4. The divine law can be spoken of, but it is not the common law. (高等教育出版社)

  5. Truth can be known, but it may not be the wellknown truth.

  比较一下几种译文,第一个"道"字第一种译文是旧音译。第二种是新音译,都不容易理解。第三种译成"道路"好些,第四种译为"天道"更好,第五种作为句子最好,但在书中可能不如"天道",

第一章　总　论

因为全书《道德经》的译名是 Laws Divine and Human（道经和德经）。"道"和"德"为什么解释为"天道"和"人道"呢？这是有根据的。《老子》第二十五章中说："人法地，地法天，天法道，道法自然。"可见"道可道"中的第一个"道"就指"天法"的客观之"道"，也指"法自然"的"天道"，所以"道"可以解释为"天道"。至于"德"呢，指的是"法地""法天""法道""法自然"的人的主观之"道"，就是"人道"或"为人之道"。所以《道德经》可以理解为"天道"和"人道"之经。

第二个"道"字分别被解释为：1. 说出，2. 告诉，3. 表达，4. 谈到，5. 知道，各有千秋。第三个"道"字和"常"字连在一起，"常"字分别被解释为：1. 永恒的，2. 经常的，3. 永恒的，4. 普通常用的，5. 众所周知的。到底哪种解释好些？这要看作者的原意，译者的理解和今天读者的理解来决定。恐怕是个"仁者见仁，智者见智"的问题。作为译者之一，只能说我译《老子》，其实是我注《老子》，也是《老子》注我，这就是说，我不能断定老子的原意到底是什么，只能根据我自己的理解，认为什么是最好的理解，就采取什么译文了，我最喜欢第五种译文，若在书中，也可考虑改成：

> The divine law can be known, but it may not be the law you know (or wellknown to you).

以上谈的是《老子》第一句。第二句接着说："名可名，非常名。"第一句谈的是抽象的，客观的"道"，第二句谈的是具体的，主观的"名"。第一个"名"指的是天地万物。怎见得？因为第三、四句接着说："无名，天地之始；有名，万物之母。"可见"名"指的是天地万物。天地万物，开始并没有名字，一直到有了人，人才给万物取名。所以第二句第一个和第三个"名"，指的是天地万物；而第二

3

个"名"是动词,是"取名"的意思,说天地万物可以取个名字,但是名字并不等于实际的天地万物。例如老子时代认为"天圆地方",实际上地并不是方的,而是圆的。所以名字是可以取的,但名字只是个符号,并不等于实物。这点非常重要,因为现在世界上很多争论,如民主、自由、人权等,争的都是名词,不是民主人权的实质。如果真正理解了老子的"名可名,非常名",争论就可以休战了。根据实际来研究理论,可以说是老子哲学的方法论。

《老子》第一章前几句:"道可道,非常道;名可名,非常名,无名,天地之始;有名,万物之母。"可以翻译如下:

> The divine law (or truth) can be known, but it may not be the law wellknown to you (or wellknown truth). Things may be named, but names are not the things. In the beginning, heaven and earth are nameless. When named, all things become known.

"道"是虚的,"名"是实的,通过"实"的"名"来研究"虚"的"道",这是研究《老子》的方法,和西方柏拉图的"多中见一"(one in many)也有相通之处,可以进行比较研究。

上面讲了"道"和天地万物的关系。但是认识"道"也好,认识天地也好,都是人的认识,所以下面就谈"道"和天地人的关系。《老子》接着说:"故常无欲,以观其妙;常有欲,以观其徼。"因此,人应该没有主观愿望,才能客观地看出"道"内在的玄妙;又应该有主观愿望,才好观察"道"无限的外在表现("徼"是极端,边际的意思。"观其徼"就是要观察"道"极端的、无边无际的表现)。这可以用《老子》中的话来说明,子曰:"予欲无言。""无言"就是"无欲",为什么"无言"呢?孔子接着说:"天何言哉?四时行焉,百物生焉。"天

第一章 总 论

不说话,却让春夏秋冬四时运行,鸟兽草木万物生长。人不说话,没有个人主观愿望,就能在具体的四时万物中,发现抽象的生长之道,这就是"观其妙"。至于"常有欲"呢?那又可以用《诗经·关雎》中两段诗来说明。"关关雎鸠,在河之洲。窈窕淑女,君子好逑。"(一对斑鸠咕咕叫,爱在河中小洲上,姑娘啊苗苗条条,情郎和她想成双。)"参差荇菜,左右流之,窈窕淑女,寤寐求之。"(荇菜啊长短不齐,水流过左右东西,姑娘啊苗苗条条,追求她直到梦里。)君子看见春夏秋冬四时行焉,听见斑鸠流水,芹菜生焉,如果没有主观愿望,那对"道"的了解不够深入,不是无限或无边无际。但他看见斑鸠成对成双,流水抚摸荇菜,自己也想和淑女成对,那对生之道,爱之道,理解就前进了一步,对"道"表现为生长发育,追求爱恋,理解的疆域又扩大了。这就说明了"常有欲,以观其徼"。"以观其妙"和"以观其徼"是《老子》的目的论。这几句可以翻译如下:

So we should be free from desires in order to understand the internal mystery of the divine law, and we should have desires in order to observe its external manifestations.

《老子》又接着说:"此二者,同出而异名,同谓之玄,玄而又玄,众妙之门。"这几句有多种理解,"此二者"指什么?有人说指"道"和"名"。那第二句"名可名,非常名"的意思就是:"道"是可以有个名字的,但是这个名字并不等于"道",这样一来,和下文"无名,天地之始;有名,万物之母"就联系不上。因为"道"有没有名字,和万物生长并没有关系。有人又把这两句的标点改为:"无,名天地之始;有,名万物之母,"并且说"此二者"指"无"和"有"。这样把"名"当动词用,说不太通。因为取名是人做的事,"天地之始"还没有人,如何"名"法?这句不通,"此二者"也就不能解释为"无"和"有"

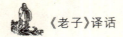

了。看来还是解释为"其妙"和"其徼"好一点,因为"妙"指微妙。就是"玄而又玄"的"玄",可见"道"的内容少而精;"徼"指边缘,就是"众妙之门"的"妙",可见"道"的形式广而大。英译文是:

> Internal mystery and external manifestations come from the same origin, but have different names. They may be called essence. The essential of the essence is the key to all mysteries.

第二章

辩证法

《老子》第一章是总论,谈到老子哲学的本体论(道),认识论(道可道,非常道),方法论(客观无欲,主观有欲),目的论(以观其妙,以观其徼)。第二章是分论,开始谈美丑善恶的相对论。第一句说:"天下皆知美之为美,斯恶矣。"在注释中,宋代范应元说:"道常无为,初无美恶。"这就是说,老子之道,原来是无所谓美恶的,四时行焉,百物生焉,都是自然之道。客观上说,四时没有美恶之分,万物也没有美恶之别,所以可说是美的,也可以说是恶的。等到天下有了人,对主观的人说来,春花秋月是美的,夏热冬寒是恶的。但美恶是相对的,如夏天炎热,似乎是恶,但五谷丰收,又是美了;冬日严寒,似乎是恶,但瑞雪丰年,又是美了。所以老子说:天下人都知道美,却不知道美恶是相对的,没有恶就没有美。如果只知有美而不知有恶,那美和恶就没有分别,美的也可以说是恶的了。第二句接着说:"皆知善之为善,斯不善矣。"也就是说,善和不善也是相对的。如瑞雪丰年对人是善事,但对冻死

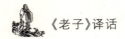

的害虫来说,却是不善的。如果认为世界上的事都是善事,没有不善的事,那善和不善也没有区别,善也可以说是不善了。下面看看北京大学出版社的译文:

The whole world knows the beautiful as beautiful only because of the existence of the ugly. The whole world knows the good as good, only because of the existence of the bad.

译文说:全世界都知道美是美,只是因为有丑恶的存在;全世界都知道善是善,只是因为有恶的存在,译者加了"只是因为"几个字,译文就容易理解了,因为翻译的不是形式,而是内容。

第二章接着说:"故有无相生,难易相成;长短相形,高下相倾;音声相和,前后相随。"这就是说,和美恶一样,有无,难易,高下,音声,前后,也都是相对的。这几句的译文如下:

1. Hence the Being and the Nothingness (Non-being) exist in opposition; the difficult and the easy complement each other; the long and the short manifest themselves by comparison; the high and the low are inclined (complement) as well as opposed to each other; the consonants and vowels harmonize with each other; the front and the back follow (succeed) each other. (北京大学出版社)

2. For "to be" and "not to be" co-exist, there cannot be one without the other: without "difficult" there cannot be "easy"; without "long" there cannot be "short"; without "high" there cannot be "low"; without sound there can be no voice; without "before" there cannot be "after". The contrary

第二章 辩证法

complement each other.(高等教育出版社)

第一种是北京大学出版社的译文,括弧内是世界图书出版公司的译文。比较一下"有无"二字,前者似乎不如后者对称,而第二种译文借用了莎士比亚的名句 To be or not to be,意味似乎更加深远。第一种译"相生""相成"等用分译法,但"相倾"并不好懂,世界图书出版公司的译文用了 complement(相辅相成),和北京大学出版社的"相成"的译文一样,可见这几个词形式不同,内容却大同小异;而"前后相随"如果根据形式译成 follow 或 succeed,内容却不对了,因为只有后能随前,前并不能随后,但是中文意义含糊,理解却不会错,这是艺术性文字的优越性。说一可以指二,说二也可指一;而英文是科学性的文字,说一是一,说二是二,没有一点含糊,译成互相追随,变成"前"可以随"后",这样就不合理。而第二种用合译法,不管形式上是"相生""相成""相形""相倾""相和""相随",都根据内容译成"相辅相成",缺一就没有二,反而更容易理解。所以翻译《老子》和理解《老子》一样,要通过原文的形式来了解原文的内容,又要通过译文的形式来表达原文的内容,内容总比形式重要。

第二章最后说:"是以圣人处无为之事,行不言之教;万物作而弗始,生而弗有,为而弗恃,功成而弗居,夫唯弗居,是以弗去。"因此,圣人做事,不必都自己做,也不是为自己;进行教育,并不必多说话;万物生长发育,却不是圣人开发的;万物成长之后,也不属于圣人所有;圣人如果做了什么,并不觉得自己了不起,可以提出什么要求;即使有了功劳,也不认为功劳是自己的。正因为功劳不属于个人,就是大家的了,上一段讲善恶功过相辅相成,这一段更进一步,讲的是功过相反相成的辩证之理,可以翻译如下:

　　Therefore, the sage does nothing for himself, teaches not

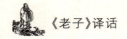

by saying, lets everything begin uninitiated and grow unpossessed, then everything is done without being his deed, succeeds without being his success. Only when success belongs to none will it belong to all.

"无为"是老子思想中的重点,但是如何理解,如何翻译?译者各不相同,如"圣人处无为之事",北京大学出版社和世界图书公司的译文分别是:

1. Thus the sage behaves without taking active action.（圣人的行为并不积极主动。）（北京大学出版社）

2. Therefore the sages do by non-action.（圣人做事并不采取行动。）（世界图书出版公司）

北京大学出版社译文比世界图书出版公司译文更容易理解,前者译的是意,后者译的是词,一般译者多于译意,但根据具体上下文看来,"生而弗有""为而不恃""功而弗居",都要是不为自己的意思,所以译成"不为个人"可能更合题意。

第三章

论无为

　　第二章谈到老子的"无为",主要是无私的意思。第三章更进一步,谈到不争名利的问题,一开始说:"不尚贤,使民不争;不贵难得之货,使民不为盗;不见可欲,使民心不乱。"这三"不"和三"民"说明了老子的政治哲学。"尚"是崇尚,崇拜的意思,"贤"指贤德的人,有德有才之士。不崇拜有德有才的人,免得老百姓争名夺位,这是第一;不看重难得的货物,免得老百姓争财夺利,偷盗抢劫,这是第二,还要更进一步,从思想上解决问题,根本不让老百姓见到所想得到的东西,免得他们利欲熏心,你争我夺,这是第三,这三点可以翻译如下:

　　Honor no man so that none would contend for honor; value no rare goods so that none would steal or rob; display nothing desirable lest people be tempted and disturbed.

　　以上是从反面说的,下面从正面来讲:"是以圣人之治,虚其心,实其腹;弱其志,弱其骨。"说圣人治理国家,

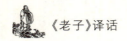

要使百姓丰衣足食,而且不胡思乱想,身体健康,但不贪图非分,这是往好处想,若往坏处想呢,那就是愚民政策,这几句的译文:

> Therefore the sage rules by purifying people's soul (simplifying or emptying their minds), filling their bellies (satisfying their needs of the stomachs), weakening their wills or ambitions (or reducing their selfish desires) and strengthening their bones (or keeping their health in good condition).

比较一下几种译文,有的往好处想,有的不那么好,很难说谁是谁非,可能是个仁者见仁,智者见智的问题。

第三章最后说:"常使民无知无欲,使夫智者不敢为也。为无为,则无不治。"关于"无知无欲",如果孤立地讲,理解为没有知识,没有欲望,那就是愚民。如果联系上下文来讲,"无知无欲"是指"虚其心"(不胡思乱想),"弱其志"(不妄图非分)来说的,指的是没有做坏事的思想,没有违反客观规律的欲望。联系下文"使智者不敢为",就是使聪明人都不敢做坏事。所以结论是:"为无为,则无不治。"只要天下都没有人做坏事,那国家还治理不好吗? 这是老子哲学思想的核心:"无为而治。"在第二章,"无为"指不为我,不为私利;在第三章,指不做坏事,不犯错误。这段可以翻译如下:

> He always keeps them knowledgeless and desireless so that the clever cannot induce them to do wrong. Where nothing wrong is done, there can be no disorder. (Act in accordance with the principle of inaction and the world will be kept in order.)

括弧中的译文不好理解。"无知无欲"还和第一章的"有欲无欲"有联系,无欲才能了解内心世界,有欲才能利用外部世界。

第四章

论道冲

　　"道"存在于内心世界,但表现于外部世界。所以第四章开始说:"道冲,而用之或不盈;渊兮,似万物之宗。""冲"字是冲虚平和的意思,一说是"盅",就是说:道是空虚的,像一个空的盅子一样,但是用处却无穷无尽,像一个永远装不满,永远倒不完的盅子;或者不如说,道是一个无底深渊,万物都是按照天道生育成长的,怎见得?老子在后面说了:"道生一,一生二,二生三,三生万物。"一二三四直到无穷无尽的万物都有生成的道路或道理,所以说"道"好像是"万物之宗"。这就说明了虚实的关系,道是虚的,万物是实的,无穷无尽的实物都是按照看不见,摸不着的道理成长发展的,这段可以译成英文如下:

　　The divine law is formless (invisibly empty, a void, empty like a bowl); its use is inexhaustible (extremely plentiful). It is endless (profound, an abyss, bottomless like a valley), whence come (spring) all things (like the originator or ancestor of

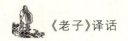

all things in the universe).

"冲"字解释为"无形的"似乎比"空洞的"好一些,因为前者指外在的形式,后者可能引起对内容的误解。"渊"字解释为"无底深渊"似乎不错,但是带有贬义,不如简单说是"无穷无尽"更好;最后一个"宗"字解释为"祖宗"也太具体,而原文是两可的,所以不如从简。

下面一段(马王堆本所无)说:"挫其锐,解其纷;和其光,同其尘。"似乎是说:"道"是冲虚平和的,如果万物中有尖锐刺人的,就要挫平;有纠缠不清的,就要解开;有光彩夺目的,就要温和;有留恋尘世的,却要同情对待。总之是要冲虚平和,译文如下:

> Let the sharp be blunted, the knot be untied (unentangled), the glare (brillance) be softened, and all be humble as dust.

最后一段说:"湛兮,似或存。吾不知谁之子,象帝之先。"据注解说:"湛"是"空明"的意思、看起来似乎是存在的,就是第二十一章说的:"道之为物,惟恍惟惚。惚兮恍兮,其中有象,恍兮惚兮,其中有物。"道就是恍恍惚惚的物象,不知道是从哪里来的,但根据老子说的:"人法地,地法天,天法道,"道在天之先,自然在天帝之先了,这段可以翻译如下:

> Apparent, it seems to exist. I do not know whence it came, it seems to have existed before God (Emperor of Heaven).

天帝可以借用西方的上帝,《圣经》中说:上帝开天辟地,所以上帝先于天地,但是西方没有"天法道"的说法,上帝只是人所取法的具体形象,而老子却抽象化为"道"了,这是中西方的不同。

第五章

论不仁

第四章谈道,道是冲虚平和,不偏不倚的,"道法自然",天地法道,人法天地。所以天地人都要法道,都要法自然,都要不偏不倚,因此第五章开始说:"天地不仁,以万物为刍狗。"就是说天地对人和对万物一样,不偏不倚,没有偏爱,把人和万物都一视同仁,对人像对其他动物和植物一样。"刍"是一种植物,是用来喂牲畜的草;狗在这里代表动物。"刍狗"还有另外一种解释,说是用草束成狗形。祈雨时当祭品,祭祀后就不用了,那天地对人就像对祭品一样只是利用而已,并没有什么仁心,这种解释不如前一种好。第五章接着说:"圣人不仁,以百姓为刍狗。"这一点老子和孔子就大不相同,孔子重仁,老子却说"圣人不仁。"为什么呢?因为人法天地,既然天地"不仁",那圣人要法天地,对百姓也要不偏不倚,这就是儒家入世、道家出世的不同之处,这两句可以译成英文如下:

Heaven and earth are indifferent (merciless, inhumane, show no bias); they treat everything like

straw or dog (straw dogs, worthless straw-dog sacrifices, let all things grow naturally). The sage is indifferent; he treats everyone like straw or dog (let the people develop themselves).

比较一下几种译文,"不仁"可以解释为 1. 冷漠不关心,2. 无情,3. 无人性,4. 没有偏见。可能第一种和第四种译文更符合不偏不倚的精神。"刍狗"的理解是:1. 刍或狗,2. 刍狗,3. 没价值的刍狗祭品,4. 让人自由发展。可能第四种最能传达原文的意思。

第五章接着说:"天地之间,其犹橐龠乎?虚而不屈,动而愈出,多言数穷,不如守中。"橐是风箱,龠是箫管,中间都是空的。老子把天地比作风箱和箫管,因为天和地之间也是空的,空虚的。"虚而不屈"的"屈",据严复说是"掘"的意思,"不屈"就是掘之不足用之不竭。"动而愈出"是说你越拉动风箱,风箱出风越多;你越吹箫管,吹出的音乐也越多,天地法道,老子把"道"比作风,说"道"在天地之间,虽然空虚抽象,但是用之不尽,取之不竭。最后八个字"多言数穷,不如守中。"和上文联系不大,湖南马王堆出土的《老子》没有这八个字,勉强解释,元代吴澄说:"数,速也。"这就是说:话说得越多,就穷竭得越快,所以不如保守中庸之道,或者学习中间空虚的风箱和箫管,说话不要太多,但是这和上面说的"虚而不屈,动而愈出"(空虚却发掘不完,动嘴说话越说越多,没完没了),不是矛盾了吗?现在看看翻译能不能解决问题:

Are not heaven and earth like a pair of bellows or a pipe? Empty, air will not be exhausted; forced, more will come out. If more is said than done, it would better to bake the mean (the void).

外文出版社译本没有译这八个字,可能是更好的解决方法。

第六章

论空灵

第四、五、六章谈的都是"道"。但却用实例来说明空虚的道总是用之不尽,取之不竭的,第四章把道比作无底深渊,第五章把取法于"道"的天地比作中间空虚的风箱和箫管,第六章又把"道"比作空空的山谷。一开始说:"谷神不死,是谓玄牝。"神是神灵,把"道"比作空谷的精神,看起来虽然空空的,但谷中万物却生生不息,永远不停。山谷就是玄妙的母亲,"道"则是"玄牝"(玄妙的母性)下面看看两种译文:

  1. The Valley Spirit or the God of Vacuity never dies, which is the profound mystery of maternity.(世界图书出版公司)

  2. The vale spirit never dies, it is the mysterious womb.(高等教育出版社)

第一种译文的"母性"译得容易理解,第二种译文更形象化,把山谷比作神秘的阴户,如果不加注释,理解就不容易了。

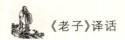《老子》译话

第六章接着说:"玄牝之门,是谓天地根。"宋代范应元注:"门者,指阴阳也,以其一开一合往来不穷而言也。"这句可以算是"地法天,天法道"的注解,上面说了:"道"是玄妙的母性,就是阴阳之道。古代把天看作阳性,把地看成阴性,天地阴阳交配,就生出了万物,所以说"道"是"天地根""人法地",也是男女阴阳交配、生生不息,因此,"天地根"包括了人的根源在内。这是老子的生命哲学,可见古人两千多年前的思想,比同时的西方神学高明得多。第六章最后说:"绵绵若存,用之不勤。"就是说"道"绵延不断,仿佛永远存在,用之不尽,取之不竭。这几句也有两种译文:

1. The opening of profound maternity is the root of Heaven and Earth. It is continuous, and its function is eternal. (世界图书出版公司)

2. Then door to the mysterious womb is the origin of heaven and earth. It lasts as if it ever existed; when used, it is inexhaustible. (高等教育出版社)

上一句的世界译文是意译,这一句是直译。不如上句好懂,高等教育出版社译文的"门"字也是直译,如指阴户倒是形似,但意思并不明确,"根"字解释为"根源",比世界图书出版公司的译文好懂一点,但不如把全句改成:

Form the mysterious womb (or from the mystery of maternity are born (or come) heaven and earth.

第四至六章几个例子都说明老子说的:"人法地,地法天,天法道,道法自然。"人取法于空谷深渊,可以说是人法天地;空谷生长万物,并且生生不息,可以说是天地法道,用之不尽,取之不竭。至

第六章 论空灵

于人用风箱,人吹箫管和道有什么关系呢?风箱中间是空的,人拉风箱,越拉风越大,只要人拉,风永远吹不完,这就是人法天地,天地法道了,箫管中间也是空的,人吹箫管就像风吹过高山低谷,森林草原,发出各种乐音,这就是人法道,道法自然了。

第七章

论无私

前几章谈空虚无为,"无为"有人理解为无所作为,有人理解为无为而无不为,也有人理解为无我,有所作为都不是为我,这就是无私了,第七章说:"天长地久,天地所以能长且久者,以其不自生,故能长生。""以其不自生"是什么意思呢?从不同的译文看来,有不同的解释:

  1. Heaven is eternal and earth everlasting. They can be so just because they do not exist for themselves. And for this reason they can long endure. (外文出版社)

  2. Heaven and earth exist for ever. The reason why they exist so long is not that they want to exist; where there is no want, to be and not to be are one. (高等教育出版社)

外文出版社采用分译法,说天是永恒的,地是长存的。其实原文天长地久并无分别,所以高等教育出版社采用合译法说天地是永远存在的。形虽不似,意却相同。第二

第七章 论无私

句外文出版社说:天地所以长存,因为天地并不是为了自己而存在的。把"不自生"理解为不为自己而生存或存在,虽然可以,但认为天地的存在有一个目的,只是目的不为自己而已。高等教育出版社的译文却认为天地的存在并没有目的,既然没有目的,那就没有什么可以判断存在的长短。例如建设社会主义,达到目的可能要几百年。如果没有目的,或者是个不可知的目的,那存在就可以是永远存在,因为目的永远也达不到。所以高等教育出版社的译文说:既然没有要不要的问题,那存在或不存在就是一回事了。

第七章接着说:"是以圣人后其身而身先,外其身而身存。非以其无私邪?故能成其私。"这有点像范仲淹说的:"先天下之忧而忧,后天下之乐而乐。"圣人要等天下人都乐了,自己才乐,这是"后其身";但是第一个天下人乐时,他也乐了,和第一个人同乐,一样快乐,这就是"身先"了。"外其身"是"置身事外",把个人得失置之度外,只考虑大家的得失,大家都有所得,他的所得也保存了,这就是"身存"。总而言之,就是要"无私",要和大家同忧乐,大家都乐,自己也乐了,这就是"成其私"。下面看看几种译文:

1. The sage similarly puts himself behind others; yet it turns out that he comes before others; he completely disregards his own existence, and yet it turns out that his existence is preserved.(北京大学出版社)Is it because they are not selfish that they attain what they attain?(世界图书出版公司)

2. Therefore for the sage the last becomes the first, the out becomes the in. As he is selfless, all become his self.(高等教育出版社)

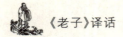《老子》译话

高等教育出版社译文说:圣人无先后内外之别,因为无私,所以公私合一了,可以说北京大学出版社的译文译的是词,高等教育出版社的译文译的是意。

第八章

论不争

第七章谈无私,第八章举实例说明,一开始说:"上善若水,水善利万物而不争。"最无私,对人和万物最好的是水,因为水给人和万物都带来好处,而不和人或万物争利,也不争夺任何东西。这一句话可以翻译如下:

> The highest good is like water. It benefits everything by giving without taking or contending (competing, vying).

水善利万物,"利"字不难翻译,就是只"给"不"取"。而"争"有三种译法,第一种是争夺的意思,括弧中的两个译文却是竞争比赛,所以不如第一种译文恰当。第八章接着说:"处众人之所恶,故几于道。"水往低处流,人往高处走,水不和人争地,(假如水要和人竞争,看谁行动更快,那就可以用括弧中的两个词。)水也不在乎高低,就往人不喜欢的低处流。而"道"则无所谓高低,所以从这一点来讲,水就接近"道"了。这一句可以译成:

《老子》译话

> Water likes the place where men dislike, so it follows closely the divine law (free from likes and dislikes).

第八章接着谈"善"的七种表现:"居善地,心善渊,与善仁,言善信,政善治,事善能,动善时。"居住的地方最好是大家不居住的低地,心最好能像空虚的深渊,给予别人最好出于仁爱,说话最好要有信用,管理最好要秩序井然,做事最好要聪明能干,行动最好不要错过时机,这七种表现可以翻译如下:

> The place should be low, the mind broad, the gifts kind, the speech trustworthy, the rule sound, the deed well done, the action timely.

第八章最后说:"夫唯不争,故无尤。"结论是:因为与世无争,所以不得罪人。不和人争地方,不钩心斗角,不患得患失,不言而无信,不争权夺位,不争名夺利,不争功邀赏。结果就没有什么过错,这个结论可以译为:

> Without contention, a man is blameless.

这里"不争"用了 contention(争夺)一词,如果改用 competition(竞赛)或 rivalry(竞争),意识就不同了,因为争夺的是成果,竞争却是要出成绩;争夺是"取得",竞争却是"给予"或"奉献",一字之差,却相差很远。老子"不争"的原意是"争夺"还是"争取"?可以仁者见仁,智者见智,到了今天,如果要把老子的思想古为今用的话,那么,"不争"的应该是名利,而不是出成绩,如果不争取好成绩,怎么能建设好国家呢?所以即使老子的原意是消极的,我们也可以利用积极的一面,何况它本来就可能有积极和消极两面的解释呢?根据自己个人的经验,如果没有国内外的翻译论战,恐怕也总结不了中国学派的文学翻译理论的。

第九章

论自满

第九章有些不同的解释,如一开始:"持而盈之,不如其己。""持"有人说是"恃"的意思,那就是说,自恃无恐,感到自满,反而不如不自恃好,而蔡志忠在《老子说》中解释说:"盛在任何器皿的水,太满了就要溢出来。"不如"八分满就够了。"把"持"理解为"拿在手里",那是本义,而且更形象化,可以译成:

Do not hold your fill but refrain from excess!

那就是说,手里拿一杯水不要太满,以免太多会溢出来。其实就是谦受益,满招损的意思。

第二句"揣而锐之,不可长保。"蔡志忠的解释是:"刀锥能用就行了,如果磨得太锐利,锋芒太露,就很容易折断。"他把"揣"理解为"磨",有人理解为"藏",可以兼顾翻译如下:

A whetted and sharpened sword, (even when hidden,) cannot be sharp for ever.

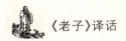《老子》译话

意思是说,磨得锋利的剑(即使藏了起来,)也不能永远保持锋利。如果不好好保存,反而锋芒外露,那宝剑就更容易损坏了。

第三句"金玉满堂,莫之能守。"这句没有什么不同的解释,三句合并起来讲,就是水不能盛得太满,剑不能磨得太锋利,金银财宝不能贪得太多,这句可以译为:

A houseful of gold and jade cannot be safeguarded.

这就是说,一屋子装满了金银财宝,怎么能保证安全,没有人来偷盗抢劫呢?

从以上三个例子可以得出什么教训?结论是:"富贵而骄,自遗其咎。"无论是水满了,还是剑锋利了,或是金玉多了,如果骄傲起来,那就是自找麻烦,这句译文如下:

Arrogance of wealth and power will bring ruin.

意思是说,不管是财富太多,或者是权力太大,都会带来祸事。总之,就是物极必反。

这是反面的教训,正面的意义呢?第九章最后说:"功成身退,天地道也。"苏东坡说:"日中则移,月满则亏,四时之运,功成者去,天地尚然,何况于人为乎!"这就是说,春夏秋冬,四时运行,日出日落,月满月亏,万物春生夏长,万民秋收冬藏,都是自然规律,功成而去,这就符合天道了,结论可以翻译如下:

Withdrawal after success conforms to the divine law.

成功之后,要退下来,否则,就不能避免物极必反的自然规律了。

第九章　论自满

外文出版社《老子》译本认为第五章最后的"多言数穷,不如守中。"应该放在第九章第一句前,有一定的道理。因为"多言数穷"和"持而盈之"(太多的话和太满的水),"不如守中"和"不如其已"(话不要太多,水不要太满)有相通之处,可以参考。

第十章

论魂魄

第九章谈到了天道,第十章又来谈人。第一句说:"载营魄抱一,能无离乎?"古代"营"和"魂"通用,"营魄"就是"魂魄","魂魄"和阴阳有联系,常说阴魂阳魄。灵魂体魄,可见灵魂代表精神生活,体魄代表物质生活。"载"是装载的意思,"抱一"是合而为一,就是说,人既有肉体,又有精神,是灵和肉合而为一的载体,但灵和肉,魂和魄,精神和肉体,有没有分离的时候呢?这就是人道的问题了。人道和天道是不是一致?有没有矛盾的时候?这句可以翻译如下:

  1. Could body and soul united never sever? (高等教育出版社)

  2. Can you keep body and soul at one with Tao? (辽宁大学出版社)

第一种译文说:合而为一的肉体和灵魂会不会分离?第二种说:你能不能使灵肉和"道"一致(或合而为一)?据老子说:"道"生万物,灵肉都是"道"生,都是按照"道"理

第十章 论魂魄

生成,所以应该是一致的。

第二句说:"专气致柔,能如婴儿乎?"晋代王弼注:"言任自然之气,致至柔之和,能若婴儿之无所欲乎?"这就是说,集中精力达到柔和,能够像没有七情六欲的婴儿一样吗?换句话说,心灵能像婴儿的肉体一样柔和吗?我们看看两种译文:

1. Can the controled spirit be softened as a baby's?(高等教育出版社)

2. Can you control your breath like a supple new-born baby?(世界图书出版公司)

第一种译文说:控制的精神(心灵)能不能像婴儿的一样柔和?第二种说:你能像柔嫩的新生婴儿一样控制呼吸(气)吗?前者指的是灵,后者指的是肉。这是用婴儿做例子,说明灵肉的柔和关系。

第三句说:"涤除玄览,能无疵乎?""玄览"是心灵的镜子,"涤除"是擦掉镜子上的污点,能使心灵没有瑕疵吗?许啸天《老子》注说:"玄览是说看通了,参通了天地间的真理(道),使心中没有一点私心遮蔽着,好似皮肤上没有瘢点一般。"可以译成英文如下:

Can the purified mental mirror be free from blemish?

译文把"涤除"理解为"纯洁化",是从正面来说;又把"玄鉴"具体化为心灵的镜子,"无疵"是指肉体的瑕疵。

前三句提出魂魄或灵肉的矛盾、柔和、瑕疵的问题,下面扩大内容,第四句说:"爱民治国,能无为(无知)乎?"一个爱民治国的圣人能不能无为(无知)而治?是无为还是无知?下面看看译文:

1. If you are to love the people and govern the state, can you avoid taking active action?(北京大学出版社)

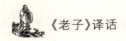

2. Can you love your people and rule your country without resorting to wisdom? （辽宁大学出版社）

3. Can a people-loving ruler not interfere in state affairs? （高等教育出版社）

北京大学出版社的译文说：如果爱民治国，能够避免采取积极行动吗？把"无为"理解为不积极行动；外文出版社的译文是不采取行动，没用"积极"二字；世界图书出版公司的译文也大同小异；高等教育出版社的译文说：一个爱民的统治者能不干预国事吗？把"无为"理解为"不干涉"。比前三种译文更加具体。但考虑到下文"明白四达，能无为乎？"重复"无为"不如用"无知"，所以还是辽宁大学出版社的译文更好。

第五句说："天门开阖，能为雌（无雌）乎？"这句解释也多，有人按照字面理解；成玄英说："天门者，心也，雌者，言其主静而和柔也。"也有人说"天门"是指天上的门，"雌"指天下人间的门，心灵之门，心灵之门（人道）应该和天门（天道）同开同阖，天人合一。哪种理解更好？可以看看译文：

1. When the door of heaven opens and closes, can you remain inactive as a female? （北京大学出版社）

2. Can you remain undisturbed by the cycles of nature? （辽宁大学出版社）

3. Can the lower doors not open and close as the upper doors in heaven? （高等教育出版社）

第一种译文说：天门开阖时，你能阴柔无为吗？第二种说：自然界天道循环，你能不受影响吗？第三种说：人间的门（人心）不能像天

第十章 论魂魄

上的门一样开关吗？以词而论，第一种最接近原文，但天门不好懂；第三种"人间的门"不加注也不好理解；还是第二种好懂一点。

第六句说："明白四达，能无知（无为）乎？"这句话也有两种版本："无知"和"无为"。"明白四达"和"无知"显然矛盾，没有知识怎能使人明白？所以这里是"无为"更好。译文也有几种：

1. Can you understand all and penetrate all without using your intelligence? （外文出版社）

2. Is it possible to understand and make understand without knowledge(by taking no action)? （高等教育出版社）

外文出版社译文说：不用智慧你能明白一切，深入一切吗？高等教育出版社译文说：没有知识（或不行动）可能明白，并且使人明白吗？是否行动好些？

最后一段："生之蓄之，生而不有，为而不恃，长而不宰，是谓玄德。"马王堆本没有这段，马叙伦认为这段应放下一章之前。主语可能是天，也可是人。说天地生养万物，并不据为己有，所以人也不应强夺天功，引以为傲，领导万物，而不主宰万物命运，这就是玄妙的道德，既是天道，也是人道。下面看看两种译文：

1. Tao gives birth to and nurtures all things. It gives birth, but does not possess; it guides, but does not dominate; this is called "mystical virtue". （辽宁大学出版社）

2. Give life and make live, but lay no claim; benefit but do not interfere, lead but do not rule. Such is mysterious virtue. （高等教育出版社）

第十一章

论有无

第十一章是谈"有"和"无"的。一开始举例说:"三十幅共一毂,当其无,有车之用。"幅是车轮上的条木,有点像今天的自行车车轮的钢丝;毂是车轮中心的空轴。车轮的三十根条木连接在车轴上,因为车轴是空心的,中心空无一物,车轮才能转动,车子才能行走,这就是"空"或"无"的作用。这句有几种译文,下面只举两个例子:

  1. Thirty spokes radiate from a hub. When there is nothing in the hub, the wheel can roll. (高等教育出版社)

  2. To put thirty spokes to form the hub of the wheel; but only when the hub is hollowed can the cart function properly. (世界图书出版公司)

第一种是意译,但"无"却是直译,否则就和主题没有联系;第二种是直译,而"无"却是意译,可能更好理解。两种译文各有千秋。

第二句再举做陶器为例,说:"埏埴以为器,当其无,

第十一章 论有无

有器之用。""埏"是陶土,"埴"是拉长,揉搓的意思,就是说用手揉陶土,做成碗或瓶子等器具,只有碗或瓶子是空的,才能用来盛饭盛水。译文也举两个例子:

1. Clay is kneaded to mould a vessel; the vessel is useful only because of the space within. (辽宁大学出版社)

2. Turn clay to make a vessel. When empty, the vessel can be used. (高等教育出版社)

"当其无",第一种译成"内部的空间",第二种简化为"空",都是意译。

第三句又举盖房子为例,说:"凿户牖以为室,当其无,有室之用。""户牖"就是门窗,建筑房屋,墙上要开窗户,房子空了才能住人。下面再看两个译例:

1. Doors and windows are cut out to form a room, but it is on the interior vacancy that the utility of the room depends. (外文出版社)

2. Build a room with doors and windows. When empty, the room can be used as dwelling. (高等教育出版社)

第一个译例把后半说成是"房子的功用要靠内部的空虚",用词文雅;第二个用词一般化。

最后的结论说:"故有之以为利,无之以为用。"从以上三个例子看来,车轮、陶器、房屋的"无",指的都是"空";那"有"指的就是"实"了。可见实物对人是有利的,但是如果没有对立的"空"或"无",实物也不能发挥作用。由此可见老子的辩证思想:有和无,虚和实,利和害,都是相对的,相反相成的。车轮、陶器、房屋等,

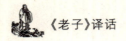

都要依靠对立的"空"或"无",才能化利为用。这句可以翻译如下:

What is useful will do good, and what seems useless may become useful.

这里把"有"译成"有用",把"无"译成"无用"。

第十二章

论声色

上一章谈"有"和"无",举的例子是车轮、陶器、房屋,都是物。这一章举的例子却是人,是人的欲望。开始说:"五色令人目盲,"说色彩斑斓,令人眼花缭乱;"五音令人耳聋。"说声音嘈杂,震耳欲聋;"五味令人口爽,"说酸甜苦辣,令人食而不知其味。总之,声色味都使人不得清静。这三句的译文举例如下:

1. The five colors may confuse the eye; the five sounds may deafen the ear; the five tastes may spoil the palate. (高等教育出版社)

2. Too much color dazzles the eyes; too much music deafens the ear; too much eating and drinking destroys the appetite. (世界图书出版公司)

第一种是直译,第二种是意译,可能意译更好理解。

下面接着说:"驰骋畋猎,令人心发狂。"这就是由静而动。由外而内,说到骑马打猎,弯弓射箭,令人心狂意乱,一发不可收拾。又说:"难得之货,令人行妨。"这又由

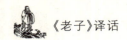

人及物,谈到金银财宝,引起贪欲,产生贪污行为,妨碍做人的品德了。这两句有几种译文:

1. Riding and hunting make man wild with excitement; rare goods goad man into stealing. (北京大学出版社)

2. Chasing and hunting may madden the mind; rare goods can lure the heart (tempt people to rob and steal). (辽宁大学出版社)

3. Overindulging in hunting drives you crazy, and coveting too much material things tarnishes your conduct. (世界图书出版公司)

"驰骋畋猎"第一、二种都是直译,第三种理解为"纵情畋猎"却是意译。"令人心发狂"第一种译文最好,第二种接近直译。第三种用词略重。"令人行妨"的译文各不相同:第一种说煽动人去盗窃,第二种用了"引诱"或"诱惑",第三种说贪图非分之财会玷污人的品行。可以说是百花齐放,各有千秋。

最后的结论是:"是以圣人为腹不为目,故去彼取此。"这就是说,圣人治国,只要人民丰衣足食,安居乐业,不要沉湎于声色犬马之乐。这就是老子清静无为的治国思想。结论的几种译文如下:

1. Thus the sage does not satisfy his eyes with colors but satisfy his stomach with enough food (governs his people by attending to their stomachs, not their senses). He discards the former and takes the latter (rejects one and accepts the other). (北京大学出版社,辽宁大学出版社)

2. Therefore, the sage is only interested in not suffering

第十二章　论声色

from hunger or starvation, but not in physical pleasures. In accordance, you should fend off material temptation and be content to live a simple life. （世界图书出版公司）

第一种译文是直译意译并用,第二种主要是意译。老子静心寡欲的思想在中国历史上起了一定的作用,但却阻碍了经济的发展。

第十三章

论荣辱

第十二章谈到人的欲望,第十三章谈对人和对自己的态度。第一句说:"宠辱若惊,贵大患若身。"这句话有两种解释:一种说:得到好评或者受到批判,总会感到不安,仿佛大难临头一般,那是把荣辱看得和身家性命一样重要了,也是把"贵"当作动词。另一种解释把"贵"当作名词,和"患"相对,说荣辱会扰乱心灵,富贵和祸患却会影响身体。下面看看译文:

1. Praise and blame disturb the mind; fortune and misfortune affect the body.(高等教育出版社)

2. Praise and blame disturb the mind for they are considered not as great trouble but as treasure as dear as one's body or life.

第一种译文把"贵"当作名词,古人有这样理解的;第二种译文当作动词,这是现代人的看法,哪种解释好些,要看下文再说。

第二句说:"何谓宠辱若惊?宠为上,辱为下,得之若

第十三章 论荣辱

惊,失之若惊,是谓宠辱若惊。"为什么说荣辱使人不安?好评使人向上,感到高兴;批判使人垂头丧气,感到痛苦,都会不安。译文如下:

> Praise and blame are like ups and downs. The mind is troubled with rise and fall, so is it troubled by praise and blame (so will it feel happy when praised, and downcast when blamed).(高等教育出版社)

译文说:好评和批判会使人感到上下升沉,高低起落,心灵会受到外界的影响,自然也会随着赞扬和批评而波动。

第三句说:"何谓贵大患若身?吾所以有大患者,为吾有身,及吾无身,吾有何患?"荣辱都是祸患,为什么要把这种祸患看得像身家性命一样重要?这是因为我老想到自己,如果我不想到自己,哪会有什么祸患呢?两种译文是:

1. How can fortune and misfortune affect the body? Because we have a body. If we had not a body, how could we be affected?

2. How can praise and blame be considered not as great trouble but as treasure as dear as one's body or life? It is because he has a body. If he had not a body, how could he feel troubled?

第一种译文把"贵"当名词,第二种当动词,两种都说得通。

最后的结论说:"故贵以身为天下,若可寄天下;爱以身为天下,若可托天下。"这里的"贵"显然是个动词,说可贵的是,重要的是,要把自己看成天下的一分子,把天下看得和自己一样贵重,一

39

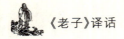

样重要;最好能爱天下像爱自己一样,那就可以把天下交托给这种人了。结论就是"无私"二字,译文如下:

> If you value the world as your body, then the world may confide in you. If you love the world as your body, then the world may be entrusted to you.

第十四章

论道纪

只有无私,才有可能得"道"。这一章又来谈"道",说"道"是看不见,听不到,摸不着的。头三句说:"视之不见名曰夷,听之不闻名曰希,搏之不得名曰微。"看不见的是消失了东西,听不到的是静寂的声音,摸不着的是微乎其微的质量。这三句翻译并不难:

> What cannot be seen is invisible. What cannot be heard is inaudible. What cannot be touched is intangible.

看不见,听不到,摸不着是"道"的三个特点。第四句说:"此三者不可致诘,故混而为一。"这三个特点是不可以分别问为什么的,合起来看,无色,无声,无形的就是"道"。这句也不难翻译:

> These three, unfathomable (indefinable), blend into one.

"不可致诘"有人说是"不可下定义的",那是回答"什么的问题;有人说是"深不可测的",那是回答"为什么"的问题,可能更有深度。下面就来回答问题:"其上不皦,其下不昧。"从文字上看来,是说从上面看"道","道"并不是明白如昼的;从下面来看,"道"也不是一片黑暗的。其实不必分开,合起来看,就是说"道"无论上下内外,一眼看来,既不是容易明白,也不是糊里糊涂的。这既不下定义,也不说出原因,而是描写说明。既不回答"道"是什么(What),也不解释为什么有"道"(Why),而是说明"道"是怎么样的(How)。这是中国哲学的艺术性和西方科学性的不同之处。译文可有两种:

1. Up, it is not bright; down, it is not dark.
2. Up and down, it is neither bright nor dark.

这是抽象的描写,下面更具体一点说:"绳绳兮不可名,复归于无物。"古代结绳记事,但是无论多少绳子,也记不清楚什么是"道",因为"道"不是物。这句可以翻译如下:

Like a nameless endless string it ends in nothing.

接着又详细地描写"道"说:"是谓无状之状,无物之象,是谓惚恍。"这就是说,"道"的形状就是没有形状,"道"的形象就是空无一物,恍恍惚惚,如有如无,翻译"惚恍",可以利用莎士比亚的名句:

It is a formless form, an image of nothing. It seems to be and not to be.

下面又从空间上来描写"道":"迎之不见其首,随之不见其后。"迎面看"道",看不见它的面目,紧紧跟随,也看不清它的背影。译文是:

第十四章 论道纪

Before it you cannot see its front; after it you cannot see its rear.

最后从时间上来描写"道":"执古之道以御今之有,能知古始,是谓道纪。"把古代的道理应用到今天的现实上,就可以博古通今,这就是应用"道"的规律(方法)。结论可以翻译如下:

Ruling over the present with the laws of the past, you can understand history ancient and modern. Such is the divine law.

第十五章

论识道

第十五章第一句有三个不同的版本:"古之善为道者(士者,上者)"到底哪个好呢?下面接着说:"微妙玄通,深不可识。""微"是精细入微,"妙"是意外地好,"玄"是深奥莫名,"通"是贯穿时空。这几个字形容"道"更合适,但从全句看来,说是得"道"的知识分子或领导人,也无不可,现在看看译文:

> The ancients followed the divine law, subtle, delicate, profound and communicative, too deep to be understood.

若从译文来看,还是"为道"更好。下面接着说:"夫惟不可识,故强为之容。"说正因为不好理解,所以勉强来形容一下。因此还是指"道"比指人更合理。从译文来看,也是如此:

> Not objectively understood, it can only be subjectively described.

第十五章 论识道

译文在"可识"前加上"客观",在"容"前加上"主观",可能更好理解。以下七句都是主观描写:"豫兮若冬涉川,犹兮若畏四邻,俨兮其若客,涣兮若冰之将释,敦兮其若朴,旷兮其若谷,混兮其若浊。"看来似乎是先描写人,后描写"道"。先说寻"道"的人犹豫不决,好像冬天要过结冰的河,或者处在四面包围之中,或者拘谨不安,像陌生的客人。接着就写寻"道"人的心情像冰一样慢慢化开,自然也可以用冰化水来象征"道"为人所理解。"道"像没有雕琢的玉石一样纯朴,像万物生长的山谷一样无边无际,像兼容并包的河水一样若清若浊。这些和西方哲学大不相同的艺术描写可以翻译如下:

> The ancients were circumspect as if they were crossing a frozen river, watchful as fearful of hostile neighbors, reserved as an unacquainted guest, softened as a melting ice, natural as uncarved block, and obscure as a muddy stream.

译文不能既说是人,又说是"道",只能全说是人。这也可以看出西方文字的科学性和严谨性,和中国文字的艺术性和灵活性大不相同。既然"道"是兼容并包,若清若浊的,能不能化浊为清呢?原文接着问道:"孰能浊以静之?徐清。孰能安以动之?徐生。"谁能使浊水变清呢?那要慢慢地来。谁能使死水流动呢?也要慢慢起死回生。这两句可以翻译如下:

> Who could calm the turbid water? It could be slowly turned clean.
>
> Who could stir the stale water? It could be slowly revived.

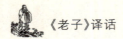《老子》译话

最后的结论说:"保此道者不欲盈。夫惟不盈,故能蔽而新成。"这几句话似乎是说:得道不能自满,也不能走极端,才能去旧立新。这个理解没有把握,只能试译如下:

Those who follow the divine law will not feel they are full to the brim. Only those who do not go to excess can renew what is worn out.

第十六章

论常道

上一章详细形容了"道",这一章综合起来,一开始说:"致虚极,守静笃。"上一章最后说"不欲盈","盈"的对立面是"虚",要达到极端的空虚,才能"万物静观皆自得"。这两句可以翻译如下:

Do you utmost to be empty-minded and hold fast to tranquility.

下面接着说:"万物并作,吾以观复。"万物同时生长发育,我静心地观察大自然的循环往复。这两句的译文可以是:

All things grow, and I see them return to nature.

接着还谈万物:"夫物芸芸,各复归其根。"万物种类繁多,千差万别,千变万化,但是万变不离其宗,不能违背发展的规律。这规律就是"归根",译文如下:

Multiple as things are, they return to their root.

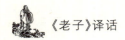《老子》译话

接着就是四个推论:"归根曰静,是谓复命,复命曰常,知常曰明。""归根"包括生长发育,开花结果,落叶归根,循环往复,由动到静。所以根就是静,归根就是由动到静,循环往复是万物发展的命运,所以说是"复命";循环往复又是符合自然规律,经常发生的现象。所以"复命"就是"常规"。知道这个常规就是聪明,智慧,就是得道,所以说"知常曰明"。这四个推论可以翻译如下:

> Their root is tranquillity; to return to it is their destiny; to submit to their destiny is the rule; to know the rule is wisdom.

这就是老子的知识论。和西方《圣经》中上帝禁止人吃智慧之果的比喻有同有异,相同之处是西方比智慧为果,东方比之为根;不同的是西方禁止,东方赞美说是"知常曰明"。这也可以看出老子思想的优越,老子接着又从反面来说:"不知常,妄作凶"。就是说,不知道万事万物的发展规律,却要胡作非为,结果就会害人害己。

> Those who act against the rule would do harm to others and to themselves.

历史上西方的宗教战争造成了欧洲的黑暗时期就是一个例子。最后,老子又从正面提出了六条推论:"知常容,容乃公,公乃全,全乃天,天乃道,道乃久,没身不殆。"知道是非对错的相对规律,就能容忍不同的意见;容忍才能公正,公正才能全面完美,全面完美只应天上有,人间哪得几回闻?因为只有天道是完美的,天长地久无时尽,天道完美无绝期,这个结论的译文如下:

> Those who understand (the law of relativity) will pardon, and to pardon is justice. Justice is perfect, and

第十六章 论常道

perfection belongs only to Heaven. Heaven exists according to the divine law, and the divine law is eternal. Men may pass away, but the divine law will never.

第十七章

论治国

　　以上谈的都是"道"的理论。这一章谈的是治国之道,第一句就有几种不同的版本:"太上,不知有之。"或"下知有之。"或"下不知有之。"三个版本文字不同,内容却大同小异,都是说最好的治国者,大家都不知道有这么一个人,或者只知道有这么一个人而已,因为他是"无为而治"的。下面接着就谈次一等的治国者:"其次,亲而誉之;其次,畏之;其次,侮之。"说下面的人对次一等的治国者表示亲近,并且赞美他;对再次一等的治国者只有害怕,甚至敬而远之;对最次一等的统治者就有一点瞧不起,甚至不放在眼里了,这几句话可以翻译如下:

　　What is the best ruler? The best ruler is one of whom none knows the existence. What is the second best? The second best is a ruler loved and praised by the people. What comes next? A ruler feared by them. Still next? A ruler disobeyed.

　　为什么有人瞧不起统治者呢?下面接着说:"信不足焉,有不

第十七章 论治国

信焉。"因为人民对统治者不够信任,甚至根本就不信任,译文可以是:

> For the ruler is not trustworthy enough or not at all.

那么,应该怎么办呢?"悠兮其贵言。"因为长期以来,统治者说话都不算数,或者说得到做不到,所以应该先做后说,做到再说,那就可以"功成事遂,百姓皆谓我自然。"等到事情做完,大功告成的时候,老百姓都觉得事是自然而然做成的,国家是无为而治的,那才是治国之道。最后几句可以翻译如下:

> For long a ruler should spare his speech. When things are done, he should let people say that all is natural.

这种理想的治国者在现实中有没有存在过?在生活中很难找到实例;在古书中,却有《论语》第十五章说的:"无为而治者,其舜也与?夫何为哉?恭己正南面而已矣。"这就是说,古代的舜帝也许可以说是"无为而治"的。他做了什么事情呢?不过是恭恭敬敬,端端正正坐在朝南的王位上,以身示范而已。至于第二等的治国者能够得到人民亲切赞美的,美国的新总统第一年得到了三分之二的选民好评,可以算是第二等了,第三等的治国者能使人民害怕,那实行恐怖统治的独裁者可以归入此类。第四等的统治者得不到人民的信任,如一个制造子弹案当选的领导人,后来又全家贪污,自然会受到人民的鄙视,这简直是不入流了。至于理想的治国人虽然不容易找到,接近理想的小领导人还不是无迹可寻的。如抗日战争时期昆明有个中学,校长以身作则,给教师充分自由,结果国文教师中出了上海社会科学院院长,英文教师把中国主要经典译成英文,数学教师得了国际数学里程碑奖,物理教师成了两弹一星科学家、化学史地教师中都有院士,这也可以算是无为而治的小典型了。

第十八章

论正反

第二章"辩证法"中说到"有无相生,难易相成"的相对论。现在更进一步,谈到正反两面,相反相成的道理,一开始说:"大道废,有仁义。""大道"就是前面说的常道,微妙玄通之道,治国之道,大道行不通了,才需要做好事的"仁"人,和"仁"人做的好事,就是"仁义"之道。这句可以翻译如下:

> When the divine law is not followed, good and just men are needed.

这就是说,如果人不按照天道做事,那时才需要仁人义士,来做好人好事。换句话说,如果人人都按天道,都是好人,都做好事,那就不需要仁人义士,因为人人都是仁人义士,还需要什么呢?只需要无为而治了。这就是无为而治的理论根据。

接着又从反面来说:"慧智出,有大伪。"如果出现了聪明智慧的人,那就是因为现实生活中缺少聪明智慧的人,才有假聪明,假智慧盛行。如果不是假冒聪明智慧,

第十八章 论正反

人人都真是聪明智慧的,那就可以无为而治了,还需要什么智慧呢?这句话可以有两种译法:

1. When intelligence is needed, falsehood must have prevailed.

2. When falsehood is practised, true and good men are needed.

第一种是直译,说需要智慧出现的时候,一定是虚伪盛行一世了。意思就是:如果人人聪明,世上没有虚伪,那还要智慧做什么呢?第二种是意译,说在弄虚作假盛行的时候,就需要忠诚老实的聪明人。比较起来,第二种和上文更好联系。

上面说的是仁义和智慧,下面接着谈"忠孝":"六亲不和,有孝慈。"父母子女亲戚之间都不和睦相处,那就要提倡父慈子孝。如果父子亲属之间关系都很融洽,哪里用得着提倡慈爱和孝敬呢?这句可以翻译如下:

When the family is at odds, filial sons and kind parents are needed.

译文和上句差不多,说只有家庭不和睦的时候,才需要孝顺的儿女和慈爱的父母。如果父母子女关系都很和睦,那慈爱和孝顺都是理所当然的事,用不着特别提倡,提倡反倒说明家庭不和睦了。

最后谈到忠诚:"国家昏乱,有忠臣。"说只有在国家混乱的时候,君不君,臣不臣,人人都不尽责任,那才需要尽忠报国。如果人人尽责,人人都是忠臣,有什么必要提出忠孝呢?这句的译文是:

When the state is at stake, loyal officials are needed.

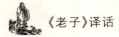《老子》译话

在国家多难的时候,才需要忠诚的官吏。如果国家平安无事,官吏各尽职责,那并不需要特别提出尽忠的问题。总而言之,老子举了仁义智慧忠孝几个例子,从反面说到正面,都是说明无为而无不为的道理。

第十九章

论弃绝

上一章从反面说到正面,这一章从上面说到下面。"绝圣弃智,民利百倍。"俗话说:"圣人不死,盗贼不止。"上面有圣人,下面就会有盗贼。因为圣人和盗贼,好人和坏人,智者和愚者都是相对的。没有好人就无所谓坏人,没有圣人就不会有盗贼,没有智者就不会有愚人。所以只要不赞美圣人和智者,世上就不会有坏人和愚人,那对老百姓不是有利无害么?这句可以直译再加补充如下:

1. If sagacity and intelligence were not praised, then people would be benefited a hundredfold. (直译)

2. If sagacity and intelligence were not praised, then people would not try to be sagacious and intelligent. There could be no bad man without the good, no fool without the wise. If no one tried to be good and wise, it would mean that no one is bad and foolish. So people would be benefited. (意译)

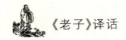《老子》译话

第二句接着说:"绝仁弃义,民复孝慈。"这句和上一句一样,说仁义孝慈等道德都是相对的,如不提倡仁义,就不会有不仁不义;不提倡父慈子孝,就不会有不孝不慈。因此,只要不提倡仁义孝慈等道德。父母对子女自然会慈爱,子女对父母自然会孝顺。这一句也可以翻译如下,就不再补充说明了。

If morality were not advocated, naturally would sons be filial and parents be kind.

第三句同样说:"绝巧弃利,盗贼无有。"这句可以有两种解释:一种和上面的一样,说巧和不巧(或拙),利和不利(或害)是相对的,没有巧就无所谓拙,没有利就无所谓害,所以不提倡巧和利,就可以避免拙和害。另一种解释说:如果上面的统治者巧取豪夺,争名夺利,下面民不聊生,怎能不被逼为盗呢?这句可以译成:

If ill-gotten wealth were rejected, no thieves or robbers would appear.

这三句由反及正,从上到下,结论是"此三者,以为文不足。"三者指圣智,仁义,巧利,文字上只提倡这三者是不够的,因为强调三者,就说明了三者反面的存在,那就是不圣不智,不仁不义,不巧不利。这句可以译成英文如下:

These three things should not be advocated in good words.

最后从正面说:"故令有所属:见素抱朴,少私寡欲,绝学无忧。"最后的结论是:第一要朴素,第二要无私,第三要无忧。无忧是对圣者说的,绝学是对智者说的;少私是对巧者而言,寡欲是对贪者而

第十九章 论弃绝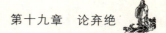

言;朴素是对仁人义士而言。全句可以翻译如下:

So the following principles should be observed: be simple and plain, selfless and desireless, unlearned and unworried.

第二十章

论独异

上一章的最后一句"绝学无忧",有的版本用作这一章第一句,说是不学习就不会忧愁,或者不必学习,不必忧愁。这和下文联系不够紧密。下文接着说:"唯之与阿,相去几何?善之与恶,相去若何?"问的是:是非之间有多远的差距?善恶之间又有多少差别?接着又从是非善恶的差别,说到别人和自己的同异:"人之所畏,不可不畏。"别人都害怕的,自己也不能不害怕。这几句译成英文是:

How far away is yes from no? How far away is good from evil?

Can I not fear what others fear? But how far are they from me?

下面接着讲自己和别人的差异,先讲别人:"众人熙熙,如享太牢,如春登台。"说大家熙熙攘攘,忙忙碌碌,好像在享受祭神的牛肉羊肉,或者在春天登台观赏风景一样。译成英文就是:

第二十章　论独异

The multitude are merry as enjoying a sacrificial feast or climbing the height in spring.

然后讲到自己:"我独泊兮其未兆,荒兮其未央,沌沌兮如婴儿之未孩;累累兮若无所归。"说我一个人漂泊无依,但是征兆并不外露,孤独荒凉,远离中心。混混沌沌,像个还没有成为孩童的婴儿,又像一累累悬空挂着的东西,没有归宿。这几句可以译成英文如下:

Alone I am so inactive as to show no sign and so far away from the center, innocent as a baby who has not yet grown up into a child, and indifferent as a homeless wanderer in the wilds.

下面继续比较众人和自己:"众人皆有余,而我独若遗,我愚人之心也哉!"说争名夺利的人似乎绰绰有余,我却受到遗弃,我的心是不是太愚蠢了! 这几句可以翻译如下:

All men have more than enough, alone I have nothing left over. What I have is a fool's heart!

最后再比较了俗人和自己,并且做出结论说:"俗人昭昭,我独昏昏,俗人察察,我独闷闷,众人皆有以,而我独顽似鄙,我独异于人,而贵食母。"俗人都清楚明白,只有我糊里糊涂;俗人都明察秋毫,只有我昏沉郁闷。众人都可有所用,只有我离群寡欢。我与众不同,因为我只看重万物的哺育者,那就是"道"。结论可以翻译如下:

The vulgar seem in the light, alone I am in the dark. They seem observant, I look dull. They are useful, I am

59

useless. Different from them, I value the mother who feeds (the divine law).

总而言之，众人欢乐而我凄凉，众人有余而我不足，众人明白而我糊涂，众人有用而我无为。简单说来，众人更重物质生活，而我更重精神生活。一句话，众人重利而我重"道"。

第二十一章

论物象

上一章谈到与众不同的论道者,这一章进一步来谈抽象的"道",开始时比较"道"与"德"说:"孔德之容,惟道是从。""道"是抽象的道理,天道,自然的规律;"德"是"道"在人(或万物)身上的具体表现,可以说是道德,本性。"孔"字有两种不同的解释:一说是空,另一说是大;"容"字既可以指内容,也可以指面容,全句是说:人的道德(或万物的本性)包含什么内容,或呈现什么面貌?这都取决于天道,都要符合自然规律。译成英文就是:

The content of human virtue conforms to the divine law.

下面就来形容"道"了,"道之为物,惟恍惟惚。""道"这种东西,是恍恍惚惚,若有若无的。译成英文可以利用莎士比亚的名句:

The divine law is something which seems to be and not to be.

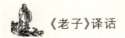《老子》译话

接着更进一步说明"恍惚":"惚兮恍兮,其中有象,恍兮惚兮,其中有物。"说"道"恍恍惚惚,有些理性知识,可以看见形象,例如方圆;有些感性知识,可以看见物体,例如方桌。这句可以翻译如下:

What seems to exist and does not exist? It is the image (idea, for example, length). What seems not to exist but exists? It is the image (or idea) of something (for example, a long table).

译文括弧中举例说明:似乎存在而不存在的形象或观念,如长短;似乎不存在的形象或观念却有存在的物体,如长桌。

除了"恍惚"以外,老子还说:"窈兮冥兮,其中有精;其精甚真,其中有信。"这就是说,从外看来,"道"是恍惚的,但是从内看来,"道"又是深奥的,"窈"是深远,"冥"是晦暗,奥妙的意思,是"道"的精神。从表面上看来,"道"是恍恍惚惚的,但是它的内在精神却是真实的,为什么呢?因为我们信"道",信仰就会产生真的力量。所以这句可以译成:

What seems deep and dark? It is the essence. In the essence we find truth, for we believe in it.

和内在的"真"或"实"相对的是外在的"名"。老子又说:"自古及今,其名不去,以阅众甫。"这就是说,从古代到现在,我们不但要知道真实,也不能没有名,因为《老子》第一章就说了:"有名,万物之母。"而"甫"就是"父","以阅众甫"就是了解万物的父母(历史)。因此,这句的译文如下:

From ancient times to present days, its name cannot be erased so that we may know the fathers (history) of all things.

62

第二十一章 论物象

老子最后说:"吾何以知众甫之状哉?以此。"他自问怎么能知道万物的历史和现状?真了解"道",就可以了解外在的物象。译文是:

How can I know what these fathers look like? By means of the divine law.

63

第二十二章

论曲直

第二章谈到辩证法,第八章谈到不争论,这一章又谈不争的辩证法。一开始谈到曲和直的矛盾说:"曲则全,枉则直。"一般人喜欢直,不喜欢曲,不知道曲和直是相对的,没有曲就无所谓直,只有直而没有曲就不够全面。举走山路为例,山路总是有曲有直的,没有弯曲的道路就不可能上山下山,就不是全面的山路,所以说"曲则全"。走弯路并不是枉费的,反而可能是两点之间最短的直路,所以又说"枉则直"。这句话可以用英文解释如下:

> A winding way may fully attain your end. It may waste your time, but is the direct way to your destination.

现在有句俗话"委曲求全",就是说从局部看来要受委屈,但从全局看来却可以达到目的。这句话有两种译文:

1. You may stoop to conquer (to win).
2. Stooping, your may fully attain your end.

第二十二章　论曲直

这句话的重点在"曲",说是"曲"才能"全"。下面又谈到盈亏、新旧、多少几对矛盾说:"洼则盈,弊则新;少则得,多则惑。"这就是说:空和满是一对矛盾,重点在空,因为空的东西可以装满;新旧也是一对矛盾,重点在旧,因为用旧了的东西可以更新。多和少更是一对相反相成的矛盾,重点在少,因为少才可以增加成为更多,多了反而会有损失,反而不知如何是好。这几句可以翻译如下:

> Something hollow may be filled up; something worn out maybe renewed. Having little, you may gain; having much, you may lose or be at a loss.

这几对矛盾说明了老子"正反合"的辩证法。直是正,曲是反,全是合。这就是说,正面的"直"和反面的"曲"统一了才更全面。盈是正,洼是反。先洼后盈就是"新"的盈,正反统一的盈。多是正,少是反,由少到多就是有所"得",就是正反的统一了。所以结论说:"是以圣人抱一为天下式。"意思是说,圣人掌握了正反合的统一,就可以用"曲""空""旧""少"来示范天下了。译成英文如下:

> So the sage holds on to "one" to be model for the world.

这个"一"(one)比柏拉图(Plato)说的 one in many(一中有多,多中见一;理论与实践,观念与现实,如"圆"的概念与"圆"的实物)更加深刻。这个理论可以应用到文学翻译上来,如"曲则全"。《红与黑》最后写市长夫人含恨而死,说 Elle mourut.(她死了。)一般译者用了"去世"二字,有的译本用了"魂归离恨天",有人认为这歪曲了原作的朴实风格,究竟谁是谁非?"去世"表示的是正常死亡,没有表达含恨而死,所以是形近实远。"魂归"字面上距离原文远,却传达了含恨而死的内容,内容是第一位的,形式风格是第二位的。因

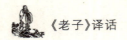

此,"魂归"比"去世"好,更加全面,这就是"曲则全"。

至于"洼则盈""少则得"的道理,下面接着说:"不自见,故明;不自是,故彰;不自伐,故有功;不自矜,故长。"这就是说,如果你有长处,不要怕别人不知道,不要有意表现自己,你越有意表现,别人越不买账,认为你是吹嘘,你越不表现自己,越不伤害别人的自尊心,越容易得到别人的承认。这就是"少则得","多则失"的说明,"不自见,故明。"可以翻译如下:

Do not show off and you will be shown up.

这句话的现实意义如何?1951—1980年我在一个外国语学院教学,学院每年评奖,总要评给德才兼备的学生。所谓德,就是全心全意为人民服务,没有私心杂念,没有名利思想,没有个人英雄主义,不喜欢自我表现。而所谓才,就是学习成绩优秀,出人头地。结果学习成绩特别好的学生很少不表现自己的,因此才高德低,评不上奖;而得奖的多是老实听话,学习并不出色的学生。这个学院的实践和老子的理论是一致呢?还是有矛盾呢?可以研究。

"不自是,故彰。"和"不自见,故明。"意思差不多,说如果你不自以为是,不总说自己有道理,别人没有道理,结果别人反而会明白你说的道理。这句的译文是:

Do not assert yourselves, and you will be asserted.

这句话的实践意义如何?实际情况也不相同,就如上面讲的《红与黑》的译例,"魂归离恨天"的译者虽然多次说明自己有理,但是赢得的读者似乎并不多;"去世"的译者也是一样,但却得到几个出版社的支持。那么,老子的话到底对不对呢?说不对吧,前者的"自是"的确没有得到更"彰"的结果,但后者却得到了。可见"自足"和

第二十二章 论曲直

"彰"并没有必然的关系。但"自是"和"是"的程度却不相同,含恨而死显然比正常死亡有理,所以"自是"的程度也更强,"彰"的程度却更弱。正常死亡不如含恨而死有理,"自是"的程度也弱,"彰"的程度却反而更高,这就说明老子有理,即使自己对了,也不必"自是"。下面两句:"不自伐,故有功;不自矜,故长。"不说自己有功,功劳反会归于自己;不自鸣得意,反会显得高大。这两句可翻译如下:

Do not talk about your success, and it will be talked about. Be not proud and others will be proud of you.

老子下结论说:"夫惟不争,故天下莫能与之争。"因为你不和别人争是非长短,高低功过,那别人怎能与你争呢?译成英文就是:

If you contend for nothing, how could anyone in the world contend with you?

最后老子又回到前面的话说:"古之所谓曲则全者,岂虚言哉!诚全而归之。"古人说的"曲则全"一点不错,非常全面。可以翻译如下:

Is it not true for the ancient to say that a winding way may fully attain the end? It is indeed the truth known to all.

第二十三章

论希言

上一章谈不争,不争自然少说,所以这一章谈"希言","希"是稀少,"言"是说话,"希言"就是少说话的意思。马王堆本不是"希言"而是"常言",并且放在上一章最后,那就和下文不连接了,不如放在这一章好。开始就说:"希言自然。"少说话是符合自然规律的。为什么呢?接着就举例说:"故飘风不终朝,骤雨不终日。"轻飘飘的风不会吹一个上午,暴风急雨更下不了一整天,而风雨就是大自然的语言,所以大自然是不太说话的。译成英文就是:

It is natural to speak little. A wanton wind cannot whisper all the morning, nor can a sudden rain howl all the day long.

轻风不能一个早上都窃窃私语,暴雨更不能整天呼喊叫嚣。接着就自问自答:"孰为此者?天地。天地尚不能久,何况于人乎!"谁使风吹不长,雨下不久的呢?回答说是天地。天地都不能长久说话,更不要说人了。这几句

第二十三章 论希言

可以翻译如下：

> Who has made them so? Heaven and Earth. Heaven and Earth cannot speak long, not to speak of men.

下面又从具体的实例回到抽象的理论。"故从事于道者，同于道；于德者同于德，于天者同于天。"所以寻求天道的人，说话做事就要符合天道；寻求道德（人道）的人，说话做事就要符合道德；取法上天的人，说话做事就要符合自然。这几句的译文可以是：

> Therefore, those who follow the divine law will conform to it; so do those who follow the human law and those who imitate Heaven.

这样做的结果呢？"同于道者，道亦采得之；同于德者；德亦乐得之；同于天者，天亦乐得之。"这就是天人合一了，寻求天道的人，得到天道，就是天人合一，自然其乐无穷，不但人得其乐，天既然和人合一，自然也得其乐了。寻求道德的人，得到道德，就是人德合一，这里把德人格化，于是就人德同得其乐了。为什么又说"同于天者"呢？因为老子说："人法地，地法天，天法道。""法"就是"取法于"的意思。老子把人所取法的分为"天地道"三个层次：道最高，地最低，天居中。三个层次都和人合而为一，都同得其乐。所以这几句可以翻译如下：

> Those who conform to the divine law are welcome to the divine, those who follow the human law are welcome to the human, and those who conform to Heaven are welcome to Heaven.

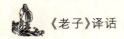《老子》译话

是不是大家都能天人合一,同得其乐呢?不是,为什么?老子说:"信不足焉,有不信焉。"因为有人不太信道,有人根本不信,所以结果不同。"希言"虽然自然,有人并不"希言"。最后的译文可以是:

Some are not faithful enough; others not at all.

第二十四章

论自见

第二十二章已经谈到自见,这一章又继续谈论。开始时说:"企者不立,跨者不行。""企"是踮着脚站起来的意思,那是站不久的;"跨"是夫跨步走路,两步路当一步走的意思,那样跨步是走不远的。这就是说,人要有自知之明,不能好高骛远,踮着脚站并不能高人一头,跨着步走也不能日行千里。这两句可以翻译成:

One who stands on tiptoe cannot stand firm, who makes big strides cannot walk long.

接着就由实入虚,从实践到理论了,第二十二章是从反面说:"不自见,故明;不自是,故彰;不自伐,故有功;不自矜,故长。"这一章从正面说,结果却是反面的。"自见者不明,自是者不彰,自伐者无功,自矜者不长。"这里有两种译文:

1. One who does not show off will be shown up, who does not assert himself will be asserted, who does not talk about his success will be talked

about, who is not proud of himself will be the pride of others.

2. One who sees only himself has no good sight, who thinks only of himself as right cannot be recognized, who boasts of his success cannot succeed, who is proud of himself cannot be a strong man (or the pride of others).

第一种译文和第二十二章差不多,第二种却说:只看见自己的人没有远大的眼光,只认为自己正确的人得不到承认,只吹嘘自己成就的人不会成功,自高自大的人不会成为强者。这理论性就更强了。

最后,老子总结说:"其在道也,曰余食赘行,物或恶之,故有道者不处。"从道的观点看来,自见、自是、自伐、自矜,就像是吃剩的食物,或者多余的行动,是令人讨厌的东西,所以懂得道理的人是不会这样做的。译成英文就是:

In the light of the divine law, such behavior is like superfluous food. It is disliked by those who follow the divine law.

总的看来,不要自我表现,不要自以为是,不要自认有功,不要自高自大。总之,就是要与世无争,这是道家的消极哲学,在中国历史上影响很大,带来了中国的太平盛世,但和中国的贫穷落后,也不是没有关系。问题在于:如果自己真是高大,真是有功,真是正确,真该表现,那应该如何呢?反观20世纪的美国所以能称雄世界,其哲学思想和老子思想基本是对立的。美国人喜欢表现自己。坚持意见,争强好胜,自认世界第一。甚至今天,美国总统奥巴马还不接受世界第二的地位。至于美国造成的世界金融危机,不是因为违反了老子哲学,而是在"义利之争"中重利轻义,不合儒家思想。所以今天我们应该在中西儒道相结合的基础上发展。

第二十五章

论大道

这是老子讲道最重要的一章。什么是"道"?"有物混成,先天地生。"老子说:开天辟地之前,只是一片混沌,这片混沌是怎么样的?"寂兮寥兮,独立不改。""寂"是寂静无声,"寥"是辽阔无边。为什么寂寥呢?因为它是独立无依的;有多么辽阔呢?辽阔得无法改变,加一分不会嫌太长,减一分不会嫌太短,这是讲混沌的形成。它会不会运动呢?"周行而不殆,可以为天地母。"它的运行是不会停止的,按照它运行的规律就形成了天地,所以可以说它是天地的父母,是开天辟地的创造者。能不能给它取个名字呢?"吾不知其名,强字之曰道,强为之名曰大。"我们不知道它的名字,就说它是"道"(道理,真理,规律),并且勉强在"道"前加一个"大"字,那就是"大道"了。这段话可以翻译如下:

There was chaos before the existence of heaven and earth. Void and vast, independent and changeless, moving in circle, it is the mother of heaven and earth. I

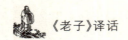

do not know its name but call it the divine law, and perfunctorily style it as great.

老子接着解释说:"大曰逝,逝曰远,远曰反。""逝"指运行,周而复始,有往有复,往就是"逝","远"指无边无际,"反"指循环往复,这就是说,大道运行,无远不至,周而复始。译成英文就是:

What is great will circulate, what circulates will go a long way, and what goes a long way will return in the end.

下面接着又说:"故道大,天大,地大,人亦大,域中有四人,而人居其一焉。"既然道的运行无边无际,自然是大;而道是天地之母,天地运行,按照无边无际之道,自然也大。为什么说"人亦大"呢?老子最后解释说:"人法地,地法天,天法道,道法自然。"人的生活取法于天地,是按照大道进行的,所以也成了"四大"中的一大。孔子说过一句话,可以作为这个道理的注解。他在《论语》中说:"天何言哉? 四时行焉,百物生焉。"天不说话,但是春夏秋冬,四时不断运行;地取法于天,万物春生夏长,秋天结果,冬天落叶;人又取法于天地,日出而作,日入而息,春耕夏种,秋收冬藏,生老病死,顺应自然。这是古人的世界观和人生观,可以翻译如下:

So the divine law is great, so are heaven and earth, and so is man. There are four beings great in the universe, and human being is one of them. Man imitates the earth, which imitates heaven, and heaven follows the divine law, and the divine law follows nature.

中国人顺应自然,成就了几千年的华夏文明。西方人更重征服自然,造成了生存竞争,优胜劣败的世界。因此中西双方应该取长补短,共同创建和平幸福的文明。

第二十六章

论轻重

　　大道是抽象的,现实是具体的,抽象的轻而上,具体的重而下。上一章谈了抽象的大道,这一章再谈轻重的关系。"重为轻根,静为躁君。"宋代范应之注:"重可载轻,静可制动。故重为轻之根,静为躁之主。"这就是说,重的东西可以装载、负担起轻的东西。静的东西可以管制、指挥动的东西,所以说重是轻的根基,冷静是躁动的控制者。另一种解释说:"重谓己身,轻为天下,身治而后天下治,故云重为轻根,躁者多欲,惟静足以制之,故云静为躁君。"重的是自己,轻的是天下,先要管好自己,才能管好天下,所以说个人是天下的根基;行动急躁的人欲望太多,想做的事太多,需要冷静的人来管制,所以说冷静可以控制急躁。第三种解释从理论和实际的观点来看,说抽象的道理是轻的,具体的现实是重的,现实是理论的基础,所以说"重为轻根"。轻重和动静有什么关系呢?一般说来,静的比动的轻,动的比静的重,而躁动就更重了。冷静才能行动,所以说静可以制动;冷静更可以制止

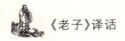《老子》译话

躁动,是躁动的制止者、管理者,如果把躁动比作臣民,那冷静就可以比作君主,所以说"静为躁君"。这两句可以翻译如下:

  The heavy is the base of the light; the still is the lord of the rash. (To be still can prevent to be rash.)

后半句的译文如果不加注解,可能不好理解。下面接着说:"是以圣人终日行不离辎重,虽有荣观,燕处超然。"范应元解释说:"君子终日行不离辎重;虽有荣华之观,亦安居而超然不顾。此比君子不离重与静也。"这就是说,领导人一天到晚进行精神活动,都不能离开物质基础,虽然看到荣华富贵,却能安然自处,超然于浮华虚荣之外。这几句可以翻译如下:

  So the sage goes on all the day long without leaving his heavy baggage (people and things to take care of). Though with glory in view, he stays light-hearted.

于是又联系实际说:"奈何万乘之主而以身轻天下?"为什么一个有万乘兵车的君主,去把个人安危看得比天下还更重要呢?译文是:

  Why should a ruler of ten thousand chariots make light of his country?

最后下结论说:"轻则失根,躁则失君。"范应元说:"人士轻忽慢易,则失根本之重,躁动多欲,则失为君之德。故人君不可须臾而离于重静也。"把国家看得比个人还轻,忽视国事,怠慢国政,以为事事轻而易举,就会失掉国家的基业;轻举妄动,三心二意,朝令夕改,不能控制自己,那就不是为君主之道了,结论可以翻译如下:

  Light, the base will be lost; rash, a ruler will be at a loss.

第二十七章

论善行

上面说了圣人为君之道,不能轻举妄动,而要物质上不离开重,精神上不离开静。下面再来说明怎样才算做得好,说得好,才算善行善言。"善行无辙迹,善言无瑕谪。"做得好要不留下痕迹,忘掉你做过的好事,说得好要不伤人,不说长道短。这是从反面来解释正面,用"重"来解释"静",译成英文就是:

> Good deeds leave no traces; good words exclude mistakes.

下面更具体说明做得好的事:"善数不用筹策,善闭无关楗而不可开,善结无绳约而不可解。"这就是说,会计算的人不需要筹码,会关门的人不需要上锁而外人进不来,会团结的人不需要用绳子也难分开。这说明的是物质和精神的关系,也是从反面来说正面。没有物质而有精神也能做得好,可见精神重于物质。这几句可以翻译如下:

> Good at counting, you may need no counters. If you know how to close, an unlocked door cannot be

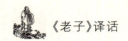

opened. If you know how to tie things up, you may make a knot without a string, which cannot be untied.

于是老子下结论说:"是以圣人常善救人,故无弃人;常善救物,故无弃物,是谓袭明。"这个结论和上文关系不紧密,有的本子删了。如果解释的话,可以说是:圣人会帮助人,不抛弃任何人;会利用一切东西,而不浪费任何东西。这就是传统的聪明,可以翻译如下:

Therefore, the sage is good at helping people without rejecting anyone, and at saving all things without abandoning anything. This is called invisible wisdom.

接着又解释说:"故善人者,不善人之师;不善人者,善人之资。"这就说明了圣人帮助人的方法,他把不善的人教育成为善人,所以他是不善人的老师,不善人是转变成善人的材料。译成英文就是:

Thus a sage is the teacher of the common people, and the common people are the stuff for good men.

最后又下结论说:"不贵其师,不爱其资,虽智大迷,是谓要妙。"如果不看重一个人的老师,如果不喜欢把普通人教育成好人,那么聪明人也会变糊涂了。这是很重要的诀窍,这个结论可以翻译如下:

If the teacher is not honored and the stuff not valued, even a wise man will be at a loss. This is an important secret.

总起来看,第二十七章可以分为两段。前五句是一段,讲善行,善言,善数,善闭,善结,这五善的精神和物质,整体和部分,正面和反面的关系。后几句是一段,从正面和反面讲善救人和善救物是传统的聪明,又讲圣人和不善人的师生关系,再讲不善人和善人的转化的关系。从这一章中可以看出老子的辩证思想。

第二十八章

论知守

老子的辩证思维还表现在知和行的关系上：知识要求高标准，行动却要求保守低姿态。因此第二十八章说："知其雄，守其雌，为天下溪。"对一件事的知识要求雄厚，像溪头活水一样源源不断，但行动却要像小溪一样缓慢平稳。小溪是水道，所以也可理解为道路，说"知高守低"是天下之道。这句可以翻译如下：

> Know as much as a strong man and keep as little as a meek wife so that you may be an endless stream in the world.

在我看来，这句话有点像英文的"希望最好，准备最坏"（Hope for the best and prepare for the Worst），如果能够准备接受最坏的结果，那就立于不败之地，这是一条用之不尽，取之不竭的原则。下面接着说："为天下溪，常德不离，复归于婴儿。"如果遵循天下的常道，那就不会离开自然的品德。人最自然的品德是婴儿的啼笑，所以像小溪流入大河，大河流入海洋，江河海洋蒸发为云为雨，又回

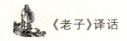

《老子》译话

到溪水源头一样，人也复归为啼笑的婴儿了。这句可以翻译如下：

> Such an endless stream will not depart from its way but return to its source in the end, as manhood will return to childhood.

第二段说："知其白，守其黑，为天下式。"这段和前段差不多，前段"知雄守雌"谈的是刚柔的内容，这段"知白守黑"谈的是光暗的外表。知道事情的光明面，自己不要争光，而要退在暗处，这样才可以做天下人的模式。下面接着说："为天下式，常德不忒，复归于无极还。"做天下的榜样，品德不出差错，不是争光，而是增光，结果反而会是无限光明，这两句的英译文是：

> Know the bright and remain in the dark so that you may be a model for the world. A model for the world will not go astray from its way but spread light without end.

第三段说："知其荣，守其辱，为天下谷。"这段的"知荣守辱"和前段的"知白守黑"也差不多，不过黑白更客观，荣辱更主观。意思是知道什么是荣誉，但是自己不去争名夺位，而愿忍辱负重，不去攀登高峰，而愿处于低谷。为什么呢？"为天下谷，常德乃足，复归于朴。"谷是洼地，前面说了："洼则盈。"洼地可以充满自然的品德，纯朴的品德，所以低谷是纯朴的高峰。这两句可以翻译如下：

> Know honor and glory but remain humble as a vale in the world. A vale may be fulfilled with its virtue and return to simplicity.

最后老子总结说："朴散则为器，圣人用之，则为官长，故大制

第二十八章 论知守

不割。"纯朴是抽象的,具体化为用器。领导人用来治国定制,制度是分散的用器,纯朴的大原则却是不可分割的,译文大致如下:

> Simplicity may be diversified into instruments. The sage may use them to rule the state, but the principle is indivisible.

第二十九章

论为之

第二十九章说:"将欲取天下而为之,吾见其不得已。"这里"取"是"夺取","为"是"妄为"的意思,就是说如果想用暴力夺取天下,主观胆大妄为,不按照客观的自然规律去治理,我看是不会得逞的。就是"马上得天下,不可以马上治之"。这句可以翻译如下:

> If anyone tries to take the world by force and rule it at will, I do not think that he can succeed.

为什么呢?因为"天下神器,不可为也。为者败之,执者失之。"所谓"神器",当时的解释和今天自然不同。在今天看来,"神器"可以理解为神圣不可侵犯的江山,即使可以用暴力夺取政权,也不可能随心所欲或用暴力治理国家。如果随心所欲统治,结果一定失败,如果想用暴力掌握政权,结果也会失掉。这几句的译文大致如下:

> The world is a sacred realm not to be ruled at will or by force. Anyone who tries it will fail, and who tries to maintain his rule by force will lose his power.

第二十九章 论为之

下面接着解释为什么不能随心所欲统治国家,"夫物或行或随,或嘘或吹,或强或羸,或载或隳。"因为万物都有自己的发展规律,人也一样:有的走在前面,有的在后跟随;有的轻声细语,有的呼风唤雨;有的身强力壮,有的身体羸弱;有的坐车骑马,有的摔跤倒地。反正千姿百态,不能随意改变,这句可以译成:

> For men or things may lead or follow, blow high or low, be strong or weak, and mount or fall.

最后下结论说:"是以圣人去甚,去奢,去泰。"因此,领导人做事不能过分,不能奢望,不能要求太高。这和儒家思想有相通之处,不过儒家的结论是要走中庸之道,道家要求更低。现在先看译文:

> So the sage will not go to excess, extravagance and extremes.

为什么圣人不走极端呢?这一章似乎言有未尽之意。

外文出版社译本在后面加了一段,现在抄在下面:"是以圣人欲不欲,不贵难得之货,学不学,复众人之所过,以恃万物之自然,而不敢为。"这可能是"去甚,去奢,去泰"进一步的解释,说圣人要没有欲望,不看重难得的东西;不学别人学的东西,恢复众人做得过分的事情的本来面以保持万物的自然状态,而不敢胆大妄为。这就说明了"不可为也"的原因。现在把外文出版社的译文抄录如下:

> Meanwhile, he (the sage) desires to have no desires. He does not value rare treasures. He learns what is unlearned. He returns to what is missed. Thus he helps all things in natural development, but does not dare to take any action.

最后一句说明了万物的自然发展,自己不采取行动的理由,可能对"不可为也"的理解有所帮助。

第三十章

论兵强

这一章开始谈军事,但是并不从正面讲。"以道佐人主者,不以兵强天下。"按照天道来辅助统治者的人,不应该用军事力量在世界上逞强。为什么呢?"其事好还。"因为用军事力量的结果,一定会引起军事冲突,善有善报,恶有恶报。所以胜利者可能会成为失败者,这两句可以翻译如下:

Those who follow the divine law in serving a ruler should not be proud of conquering the world by force. For the conqueror may in turn be conquered.

军事冲突造成的破坏很大。"师之所处,荆棘生焉。大军之后,必有凶年。"军队所到的地方总会有战争,总会破坏生产,田地长出荆棘,粮食收成减少,人民生活困难,接着带来的是饥饿和灾荒。这两句的译文是:

Where the army goes, there briars and thorns grow. After a war usually comes a year of famine.

第三十章 论兵强

因此,"善有果而已,不敢以取强。"善于用兵的人只要求好结果,并不争强好胜。怎样不争强好胜呢?具体说来就是:"果而勿矜,果而勿伐,果而勿骄,果而不得已,果而勿强。"有了好结果而不要自高自大,争功求赏,目中无人,要知道好结果是自然而然,水到渠成的,所以不用巧取豪夺,勉为其难,就会得到,这几句话可以翻译如下:

> It would be better to achieve good results than to conquer by force. Good results never lead to self-conceit, nor to vain glory, nor to undue pride; they are something unavoidable, to come naturally and not to be achieved by force.

最后的结论是:"物壮则老,是谓不道,不道早已。"因为物极必反,盛极必衰,壮年之后,老年就要来到。这是不可违反的自然规律,违反自然规律却会适得其反,会衰败得更快。译成英文大致是:

> The prime is followed by the decline, or it is against the divine law. What is against the divine law will come to an early end.

中国书店出版社的《老子》第 157 页引用严复的话说:"中国古之以兵强者,蚩尤尚矣。秦有白起,楚有项羽,欧洲有亚历山大,有汉尼伯,有拿破仑,最精用兵者也。然有不早已者乎?曰'好还',曰'早已',老子之言固不信耶?至有始有卒者,皆有果,勿强而不得已也。"严复认为中国古代用兵逞强的人有和黄帝大战的蚩尤,秦国大将白起,大破秦兵的楚霸王项羽,欧洲有征服欧亚非大陆的亚历山大和汉尼伯,大败德奥英俄的拿破仑,但都没有得到好结果,早已明日黄花了。还是老子说得对,不要争强好胜,而要善始善终,这是中国以和为贵的思想。

第三十一章

论吉凶

老子反对用兵逞强,这一章再加以说明。"夫兵者不祥之器,物或恶之,故有道者不处。"因为用兵是不吉祥的事,是凶险的苦难,所以大家都厌恶战争。懂得道理的人都不愿意打仗。也可以说兵器是不吉祥的东西,造成数不清的灾祸,所以得道明理的人都敬而远之。这两句话可以翻译如下:

Weapons are tools of evil omen detested by all. Those who follow the divine law will not resort to them.

下面接着说:"君子居则贵左,用兵则贵右。"范应元注说:"左阳也,主生;右阴也,主杀。"君子就是上面说的"有道者",他们安居乐业,热爱和平生活;到了战争年代,大家自然重武轻文了。下面又重复说:"兵者不祥之器,非君子之器。"但是兵器是杀人的凶器,得道明理的人自然不用了。译成英文就是:

第三十一章 论吉凶

> A worthy man prefers the left in time of peace and the right in time of war. Weapons are tools of evil omen, not to be used by worthy men.

这说的是和平时期,到了战时怎么办?"不得已而用之,恬淡为上。""恬淡"二字,各种版本不同,大约是越少越好吧。结合下文来看,"胜而不美,而美之者,是乐杀人。""恬淡"似乎又是不要得意的意思。得意不是表示乐于杀人吗?"夫乐杀人者,不可以得志于天下矣。"喜欢杀人,怎么可能得意洋洋呢?这几句可以翻译如下:

> When they are compelled to use them, the less often, the better. Victory should not be glorified. To glorify it is to be delighted in killing. Those delighted in killing cannot win the world.

下面又谈吉凶祸福的事:"吉事尚左,凶事尚右,偏将军居左,上将军居右,言以丧礼处之。"有的版本没有这几句话,行军时,偏将在左,上将在右,因为行军作战是凶险的事,所以应该按照丧礼安排上将和偏将的位置,关于吉凶的话可以翻译如下:

> Good omen keeps to the left and evil omen to the right. A Lieutenant general keeps to the left and a full general to the right as in the funeral service.

最后再补充说:"杀人之众,以哀悲泣之。战胜,以丧礼处之。"因为战争伤亡很多,所以应该感到悲哀,应该痛哭流泪,即使打了胜仗,也不应该庆祝,而该按照丧礼,哀悼阵亡将士。这种对于吉凶的看法,译成英文是:

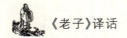

The heavier the casualties, the deeper the mourning should be. Even a victory should be celebrated in funeral ceremony.

这是中国和西方对战争与和平，胜利和失败的不同看法。

第三十二章

论道常

第三十二章谈到"道":"道常,无名之朴,虽小,天下莫能臣也。"这是关于"道"的总论,说"道"是经常存在的,是简单纯朴,无以名之的。虽然单纯微小,但是天下没有什么事能够不按照"道"(规律)进行。还有一种版本是:"道常无名,朴虽小,天下莫能臣也。"那就是把"常"当作副词,把"朴"当作"道"的同义词了。说"道"经常是没有名字的,虽然单纯微小,却不臣服于天下任何事物。两种说法大同小异,现在把两种译文抄录如下:

1. The divine law is changeless; it is nameless simplicity. No matter how little and simple, the world must follow it.(高等教育出版社)

2. The Tao is nameless for ever; though it is very small, it is subject to no one in the world. (北京大学出版社)

第一种译文说:天道经常不变,是无名的纯朴,无论多么单纯微小,全世界都不得不按照"道"的规律行事。第二

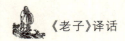《老子》译话

种译文说:"道"是永远无名的,虽然很小,却不臣服于天下任何人。从文字上看,第二种译文接近原文,但说"道"永远无名,不如说无名的纯朴,可以理解为说不出的纯朴。其次是用法问题,subject 当形容词,后面一般用动作性的名词,不用具体的人或物。所以第二种译文不如第一种。

下面接着说:"侯王若能守之,万物将自宾。"帝王诸侯如果能按照"道"理行事,万事万物都会像宾客听从主人安排一样遵守规律。这句可以翻译如下:

> If rulers can observe it (the divine law), everything will be subject to their rule.

这里 subject to 后面用了动词性的名词"统治",就合乎英文用法了。下面举例说明:"天地相合以降甘露,民莫之令而自均。"天上降下雨露,均匀地分布在地上。这是自然的规律,不是服从人的命令,所以领导者也只要按照自然规律做事就行了。译成英文大致是:

> When heaven and earth mingle, sweet dew will fall; not ordered by people, it falls without prejudice.

最后谈到有名无名的问题。第一章说过:"无名,天地之始;有名,万物之母。"这一章说:"始制有名,名亦既有,夫亦将知止,知止可以不殆。譬道之在天下,犹川谷之于江海。"天地开始无名,道生天地,天地生万物,这才开始制定名字。天地万物按照"道"的规律运行,所以一切始于道,也止于道,就像天降雨露,溶入百川,流入江海,又化为云雨,周而复始,这就是"道"。可以翻译如下:

> When things begin to be named, names come into being.

第三十二章　论道常

The beginning implies the end; the end will begin again. Thus the divine law prevails in the world just as streams formed by dew and rain flow from vales into rivers and seas.

第三十三章

论知行

上一章谈天道,有一个知和行的问题:"知"是知道自然规律,"行"是天地万物按照自然规律运行,那是天道。人也按照自然规律行动,那却是人道。人道也有"知"和"行"两方面。这一章开始说:"知人者智,自知者明。"这就是说:知道人,理解人,需要智慧;而知道自己,理解自己,那却需要聪明。"智"和"明"如何翻译?看看下列几种译文:1.北京大学出版社(外文出版社,世界图书出版公司),2.辽宁大学出版社,3.高等教育出版社。

1. He who knows others is wise (knowledgeable, witty); he who knows himself is clever (wise, wise).

2. Knowing others is wisdom; knowing one's self is insight.

3. It needs observation to know others but reflection to know oneself.

北京大学出版社的译文把"智"解释为智慧,聪明才智,把

第三十三章 论知行

"明"解释为聪明伶俐,从字面上看不错,但深入分析一下,似乎没有确切说明知人和自知的分别,因为知人和自知都需要聪明才智,而聪明伶俐的人并不一定有自知之明。外文出版社把"智"解释为有知识的,有见解的,比较好些。世界图书出版公司把"智"解释为机智,那是一种临机应变,灵活自如的才能,和知人或自知的关系不大。辽宁大学出版社的译文把"明"解释为有眼光,有洞察力,倒是不错,但是知人难道不要眼光么?如果要把知人和自知分开,可能还是高等教育出版社的译文更好:知人需要观察力强,自知需要反省思考。但是形式距离原文却又远了一点。

上面谈了"知"的问题,下面再来谈"行":"胜人者有力,自胜者强。""胜"是胜过,超越的意思,胜过别人需要有力量,超越自己却更需要精神力量,因此英文可以译成:

> Physically strong, one can conquer (surpass) others; mentally strong, one can surpass (conquer) oneself.

译文"有力"加上了"体力方面","强"前加了"精神方面",只是强调二者的分别,并不是说"胜人者"不需要精神力量。

下面把"知"和"行"结合起来谈。"知足者富,强行者有志。"人生有"收入"和"付出"两方面,就收入而言,一个人应该知足常乐,因为贫富是相对的,如不知足,永远觉得收入不够,如果知足,精神上先富了,不会觉得收入太少。就付出而言,应该立志尽量多做贡献,行动上要多多益善,那才是个有大志的强人。这句可以译成:

> Content, one is rich; with strong will, one can persevere.

最后谈到知足和强行的结果,"不失其所者久;死而不亡者

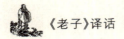《老子》译话

寿。"因为知足,总会觉得"得其所哉",生命长久,身后不会为人遗忘,精神不死,可以说是长寿了。这句可以翻译如下:

    Staying where one should, one can endure long; unforgettable, one is immortal.

第三十四章

论大道

　　第三十二章谈了道常,这一章谈大道,一开始说:"大道泛兮,其可左右。"严复说:"大道,常道也,左右之名,起于观道者之所居。比如立表,东人谓西,西人谓东,非表之东西也,非道之有左右也。"严复认为大道就指常道,大道广泛无边,上下左右,无所不包。所谓左右,是"观道者"的立场观点,你从左边看"道","道"在右边;你从右边看"道",又在左边。"道"犹如一块纪念碑,站在东边看碑的人,说碑在西;站在西边看碑的人却说在东。其实纪念碑无所谓东或西,道也无所谓左或右,而是无左无右。无所不在。译成英文可把大道比作河流:

> The divine law is a stream overflowing left and right.

大道是左右逢源的河流。"万物持之以生而不辞,功成而不名有。"天地万物都按照大道生长,运行不止,大道一视同仁,毫无偏颇,万物生长发育,开花结果,大道并不争功争名,争为已有。"衣养万物而不为主,可名为小。""衣"

是遮盖保护的意思,说天在上面保护,地在下面蓄养,万物按照自然规律生长发育,大道并不自高自大,自以为主,而是不分大小,所以大道也可以说是小道。这两句可以翻译如下:

> All things grow from it, and it never turns away. It achieves the deed without the fame. It breeds all things without claiming to be their lord. So it may be called "a little way".

另一方面,"万物归焉而不为主,可名为大。"虽然大道并不自以为大,自以为主,但是万物都是按照"道"的规律运行的,真是其大无比,所以又可以说"道"大。译成英文就是:

> All things cling to (depend on) it (All are done in accordance with the law), but it will not claim to be their master. So it may be called "a great way".

最后的结论说:"以其终不自为大,故能成其大。"说来说去,说到底,"道"并不认为自己大,结果反而成了大道。这可翻译如下:

> As it never claims to be great, so it becomes a great way.

总而言之,大小长短,上下左右,都是相对而言的,没有绝对的大小左右。而道是无所不包的,所以从总体而言,可以说是大道;具体到每一件小事,又可以说是小道。老子不赞成自以为大,因为那就排斥了小的一面。这谈的是抽象的道,可大可小。如果是具体的事物,那大小就可以有一个客观的标准,主观应该和客观统一,客观上事物符合大的标准,说那是大,应该算是实事求是;如果自己客观上不符合大的标准,却说是大,那才是自高自大。这可能是中国和西方的不同之处:中国主张谦虚,往往主观低于客观;西方发扬科学精神,要求主观客观统一,这点应该取长补短。

第三十五章

论道感

大道主要是谈抽象的理性知识,现在来谈具体的感性知识,也就是"道"的形象。"执大象,天下往,往而不害,安平泰。"这句话有两种解释:一说只要掌握了大道的形象,天下人都会心向往之;如果一心向往大道,自然不会互相伤害。于是天下太平,国泰民安。另一说是:掌握了大道就可以走遍天下,无往而不利,不会有害,天下人都会安居乐业,与世无争,平安稳定。两种说法大同小异,可以有不同的译文:

1. He who holds the great image (Tao) attracts all the people to him. Coming to him and not harming each other, they all live in peace and happiness. (北京大学出版社)

2. Keeping the great image (the divine law) in mind, you may go everywhere in the world without bringing any harm but safety, peace and security. (高等教育出版社)

大道可以使人安居乐业，但是物质上的享受，精神上的乐趣不也可以得到同样的结果么？于是这一章接着说："乐与饵，过客止。"音乐和美食也可以使听见的人，看到的人不再前进，停下来欣赏享受。那有什么不同呢？下面接着又说："道之出口，淡乎其无味，视之不足见，听之不足闻，用之不足既。""道"从口里说出来是淡而无味的，似乎比不上美食；看起来没有形象之美，听起来又没有音乐的声色之美。但是"道"和音乐美食都不同，因为天长地久有时尽，"道"却是用之而不尽，取之而不竭的。这就是"道"这个无形之象，无声之音，无味之食，胜过一切物质的和精神的享受之处。这几句可有三种译文如下：

1. Music and food can allure passers-by to stop, but the Tao, coming out of the mouth, is tasteless. It cannot be seen, it cannot be heard, but when using it, you can never exhaust its use.（北京大学出版社）

2. Music and food may attract the travelers of the world. The divine law is tasteless when it comes out of the mouth, invisible when looked at, and inaudible when listened to, but it is inexhaustible when used.（高等教育出版社）

3. Music and delicious food (dainties) make the passers-by stop and tarry. But when the great Dao is expressed in words, it will be plain or even monotonous. When you listen to it, it cannot be heard; when you look at it, it cannot be seen. However, when you apply it, it can be limitless.（世界图书出版公司）

三种译文之中，第二种更精练。

第三十六章

论刚柔

　　上一章讲了"道"是无形之象,无声之音,无味之食,讲的是形象,声音,食味的辩证关系。这一章来讲辩证法,"将欲歙之,必固张之;将欲弱之,必固强之;将欲废之,必固兴之;将欲夺之,必固与之:是谓微明。""歙"是吸气(呼吸)的意思,"张"是张开口鼻,呼吸和张口是一对矛盾,必须先张开口鼻然后呼吸,不然就无法呼吸了。强和弱是第二对矛盾,要削弱对方,一定要对方有相当的强度;如果没有一定的强度,那就用不着削弱了。第三对矛盾是兴和废,废除一事一物的先决条件,是那件事物已经兴起了;如果没有兴起,哪里谈得到废除呢?第四对矛盾是夺取(或取得)和给予,人和人的关系是互相帮助的,如果不给予帮助,自己也得不到帮助;给予的帮助越多,得到的帮助也会越多。"微明"就是黎明。如果说给予是黎明的话,得到就是白天,黎明是白天的前奏曲。其他三对矛盾也是一样。如果说"歙之,弱之,废之"是目的,那"张之,强之,兴之"就是手段,就是"微明"。这几句有不同的

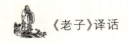

英译文：

1. Inhale before you exhale; strengthen what is to be weakened; raise what is to fall; give before you take: such is the twilight before the day.（高等教育出版社）

2. In order to contract (reduce) it, it is necessary to expand (stretch) it first; in order to weaken it, it is necessary to strenghten it first; in order to destroy (remove, discard) it, it is necessary to promote (accept, praise) it; in order to grasp (take, seize) it, it is necessary to offer (give) it first. This is called subtle light (wisdom, insight, sign faint and obvious).

第一种译文把第一对矛盾改成"呼"和"吸"，说要呼出气去，就要先吸进气来，因为在英文中，呼吸和张开口鼻不是一对矛盾；第二对矛盾说：应该加强要衰弱的；第三对说：应该振兴要衰落的；第四对说：欲将取之，必先与之。矛盾虽然都说对了，但有些目的和手段却颠倒了。第二种译文是外文出版社的，括弧中是北京大学出版社，辽宁大学出版社，世界图书出版公司的，虽然说对了，但太啰唆。如何取舍，只好各随其便了。

最后说到主题："柔弱胜刚强，"并且举例说："鱼不可脱于渊。"鱼离不开深渊的水，水性很柔，似乎不如鱼强，但是水可以离开鱼，鱼却不可能离开水。可见柔弱能够胜过刚强。虽然胜过，但是不能争强好胜，自高自大，因为"国之利器，不可以示人。"一个强国克敌制胜的武器应该保守秘密，不可向人炫耀，机密如果泄漏，优势反而变成劣势了，这几句可以翻译如下：

第三十六章　论刚柔

The soft and weak may overcome the hard and strong. Fish should not go out of water. The sharpest weapon of a state should not be shown to others.

第三十七章

论无为

无为是老子的重要思想,但是如何理解"无为"呢?晋代王弼说:"顺自然也。"很有道理。这一章一开始就说:"道常无为而无不为。"就是说"道"是顺其自然,让万物各行其是,而不横加干涉的。"道"本身无为,而让万物各尽所能,为所能为,那"道"就是无所不为了。所以"无为"的意思,是不干涉,不做错事。这句译成英文就是:

> The divine law will not do what it cannot, but let everything do what it can, so there is nothing which the divine law cannot do.

下面接着说:"侯王若能守之,万物将自化。"王公诸侯等统治者如果能按照"无为"的原则办事,不加干涉,不犯错误,那万物自然会各得其所,各尽所能,那就是无为而无不为了。这句可以翻译如下:

> If rulers can follow it (the divine law), everything will be done by itself.

第三十七章　论无为

接着又说:"化而欲作,吾将镇之以无名之朴。"如果万物顺其自然,各尽所能的时候,统治者起了干涉的欲望怎么办?那就只好用简单纯朴的无名之"道",来制止干涉的欲望。下面还重复说:"镇之以无名之朴,夫将不欲。"按照简单纯朴的道理,使统治者知道干涉并不能实现自己的欲望,不干涉而让万物各尽所能,反能达到统治的目的,这样就能制止干涉的欲望。最后下结论说:"不欲以静,天下将自定。"如果干涉的欲望能够平静下来,万物能够各行其是,各尽所能,那天下自然安定太平了。这几句译成英文大致是:

If there is desire to interfere, I will try to pacify it by nameless simplicity. How can I pacify the desire to interfere? (I will tell the ruler that interference cannot achieve his end which non-interference can.) When the desire is pacified, the world will be well ruled by itself.

由此可见无为而治是老子的重要思想。

有的版本把老子《道德经》分为上下篇:第三十七章以前为上篇《道经》,以后为下篇《德经》。第三十七章总结了"道"的思想就是"无为而无不为"。第一章是总论:"道可道,非常道"是"道"的认识论。第二章辩证法谈到的"有无相生,难易相成"是"道"的方法论。第三章谈到的"使民不争,无为而治"是"道"的目的论。第二十五章"人法地,地法天,天法道,道法自然"是"道"的本体论。其他各章多是辩证法的分论:虚实,盈亏,公私,雄雌,有无,声色,荣辱,主客,正反,是非,曲直,言行,人我,轻重,善恶,知行,取予,强弱,刚柔等等。总的看来,老子总是站在弱的一边,柔的一面,主张以柔克刚,以弱胜强。这和儒家思想"谦受益,满招损"有相通之处,不过儒家重积极面,道家重消极面,所以我们应该取长补短。

第三十八章

论　德

　　林语堂在《老子的智慧》中说:"本章乃是《老子》最著名的一章。有不少版本把《老子》这本书分为上下两篇(《道经》和《德经》),本章就是下篇的第一章。"主要谈"德"的问题。一开始说:"上德不德,是以有德;下德不失德,是以无德。"第一个"德"是名词,是"道德"的意思,"上德"就是上等的道德,或高级的道德。第二个"德"是动词,是认为自己有道德的意思。以后三个"德"字都是名词:"下德"是下等的或低级的道德,"失德"可以是失去了道德或没有道德的意思,在这里可能是"不认为自己没有道德"。全句是说:道德高尚的人总是自然地按照道德标准做事,并不觉得(或认为)自己有什么与众不同的道德;道德不那么高尚的人却不认为自己没有那么高尚的道德,结果反而成了没有高尚道德的人,这句可以翻译如下:

　　A man of high virtue does not claim he has virtue, so he is virtuous. A man of low virtue does not

第三十八章 论 德

confess he has no high virtue, so he is virtueless.

第二句说:"上德无为而无以为;下德无为而有以为。"道德高尚的人做什么事都顺其自然,没有个人目的,都是无所为而为的。德行不高的人做事都有个人目的,都是有所为而为。这句可以译成英文如下:

A man of high virtue does nothing on purpose; A man of low virtue does nothing without purpose.

下面就来具体分析德行,按照仁义礼智信五方面来讲说:"上仁为之而无以为。上义为之而有以为。上礼为之而莫之应,则攘臂而扔之。"这就是说:仁人做事是无所为而为的,没有个人目的;义士做事却是为了仗义,那就是有所为而为了。重礼的人更进一步,他自己先行礼,如果对方没有回礼,他就伸出手来,强迫对方行礼。这就是老子的道教和孔子的礼教不同之处:道教顺其自然,礼教要人循规蹈矩。这些可以翻译如下:

A good man will do good without purpose, A just man will do justice on purpose.

A ritualist performing rites without receiving response will stretch out his arms to force the man he salutes to perform rites.

第三十八章接着说:"故失道而后德,失德而后仁,失仁而后义,失义而后礼。"这就是说,如果不能按照天道,顺其自然做事,那就应该按照道德。如果不能按照道德,那就应该顺应人道,做个仁人。如果做不到仁人。那还可以做个义士,仁人可以无所为而为,不抱个人目的;义士却是做自己认为适宜的事,是有所为而为,主

105

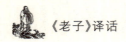《老子》译话

观程度更高,客观程度更低,这就是有所为而为了。这几句理解可能有问题,试先译成英文如下:

> When the divine law is not followed, we may resort to virtue; When virtue cannot be practised, we may resort to humanism;
>
> If humanism should fail, we may resort to justice; If justice should fail, we may resort to the rites.

这几句话有不同的解释,如刘师培说:"老子之旨,盖言道失而德从而失,德失而仁从而失,仁失而义从而失,义失则礼从而失也。"这种解释说一失"道","德仁义礼"也都失掉了。我原来按照这种理解翻译如下:

> So virtue is lost when the divine law is not followed; humanism is lost after virtue; justice is lost after humanism; formalism (or ritualism) is lost after justice.

后来觉得这种解释上下文不连贯,前后似乎矛盾,因为"礼"既然失掉了,为什么下文还要说"礼"是"乱之首"呢?我认为这一章主要讲道德和礼教的异同。道德包括礼教,礼教来自道德,道德是内容,礼教是形式。道是抽象的原理,德是万物所得于道的具体品质,仁义是人所得于道的品质,礼是仁义的外在形式。所以老子排列的次序是:一道,二德,三仁,四义,五礼。可见他对道德的重视,认为礼教不如道德重要。

他接着说:"夫礼者,忠信之薄,而乱之首。"礼是规矩,既然要定规矩,那就说明人不知道规矩,或者不守规矩。也说明人不忠诚老实,不值得信任,所以才要礼教来定规矩。如果做人不是忠诚老

第三十八章 论 德

实,做事也不值得信任、那就一定会出乱子。礼教只能治标,规矩只是表面上限制人,并不能够治本,治本还是要靠道德。老子这句话可以译成:

> Ritualism shows the loss of loyalty and faith, so it is the beginning of disorder.

礼教说明道德失败了,所以才要规矩来限制人,限制会引起反对,所以会出乱子。怎么预防乱子呢?老子说:"前识者,道之华,而愚之始。"预防要有先见之明(就是"仁义礼智信"中的"智"),先见之明可能华而不实,华而不实表面上看起来聪明,其实可能是愚蠢的开始。译成英文就是:

> Foresight (or wisdom) which is the superfluous part of the divine law, may lead to ignorance.

因此结论是:"是以大丈夫处其厚,不居其薄,处其实,不居其华,故去彼取此。"上面说"夫礼者,忠信之薄。"说"礼"是"薄",那"厚"就是"忠信",说"先见"(或智)是"华",那"实"可能是"德"。所以结论仿佛是说:士大夫要看重道德忠信,不要看重礼和智,因为礼教做的是表面工作,道德才是实际起作用的。所以要重道德轻礼教。这几句可以翻译如下:

> Therefore, an intelligentle man should be loyal and faithful rather than ritual, and be substantial rather than superfluous. He rejects not the former but the latter.

老子对孔子的礼教(或礼治)理解并不全面,因为孔子的礼治还可以在《礼记》中读到:"大道之行也,天下为公,选贤与能,讲信

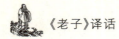

修睦。"后面还说到人尽其才,物尽其用的话。老子的道,只是"道法自然",孔子也法自然,如他说过:"天何言哉?四时行焉!百物生焉!"但他的大道是天下为公,选贤重德,选能重才。讲信修睦,和平共处。所以中国古代知识分子"穷则独善其身,达则兼善天下"其实是孔老之道并行不悖的。

第三十九章

论得道

　　上一章谈了道的重要性,这一章就来谈得道的情况。老子一开始说:"昔之得一者,天得一以清,地得一以宁,神得一以灵,谷得一以盈,万物得一以生,侯王得一以为天下正。"这里"得一"就是"得道","和道一致"的意思;用今天的话来说,就是"合乎道理",甚至是"合乎科学"。天地万物如果合乎道理,天就会清明晴朗。那"一"或"道"就指气象学了,大地如果合理,就会平安无事,无灾无难。那"理"就指地理学,地震学"神得一以灵"有两种可能:如果"神"指具体的风雨雷电,那"一"还是气象学;如果指抽象的神灵,那就是宗教学了。"谷"指谷地平原,如果种植合理,就会五谷丰收,这"一"是指农业科学,"万物得一以生",那"一"的范围更广,包括生物学,地质学。帝王将相如果懂得治理国家的道理,那就可以天下太平,这"一"指的是政治学,经济学,法学等。由此可见,两千五百年前,中国哲学已经发展到了什么地步。到了今天,我们要与时俱进,老子的话自然要取其精华,去其糟粕。这一段可

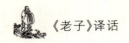《老子》译话

翻译如下：

> When one with the divine law, heaven would be clear, earth stable, spirits divine, valleys full, all creatures alive, and rulers would be praised in the world.

下面，老子从反面说："其致之也，天无以清将恐裂，地无以宁将恐废，神无以灵将恐歇，谷无以盈将恐竭，万物无以生将恐灭，侯王无以正将恐蹶。"这就是问：天地万物为什么要这样呢？因为天不清明就会雷电交加，天空开裂；地不安宁就有水旱灾荒，物不能尽其用；人不信神就会善恶不分，做坏事也肆无忌惮；谷物如果不能丰收，那收成就越来越少，最后甚至落空，不得温饱；万物如果不能生长，也就只好慢慢消灭；统治者如果不能国泰民安，就会寸步难行，走向衰败。这几句也可翻译如下：

> Why should they be one with the divine law? If not clear, heaven would split; if not stable, earth would quake; if not divine, spirits would disappear; if not full, valley would parch; if not alive, all creatures would perish; if not successful, rulers would fall.

从正面和反面说了之后，老子来总结了："故贵以贱为本，高以下为基。"贵贱高下是相对的，没有贱也就没有贵。没有下也就没有高，高是由下面一步一步走上来的，贵也是由贱一步一步提升的。所以"下"是"高"的基础，"贱"是"贵"的基础。老子又举例说："是以侯王自谓孤寡不穀，此非以贱为本邪？非乎？"因此帝王自称"孤家""寡人"，这不是表明贵族原本出自贫贱之家吗？这几句可以译成英文如下：

第三十九章 论得道

Thus the noble come from the humble and the high is based on the low. That is why rulers call themselves sole and unworthy. Does it not show that they are humble in their origin? Is that not true?

最后,老子说:"故至誉无誉,不欲琭琭如玉,珞珞如石。"所以最高的荣誉就是不要荣誉,既不要做光彩夺目的宝玉,也不要做叮当作响的石头。用英文说就是:

Therefore, too much honor amounts to no honor. We should have no desire for glittering jade nor for tinkling stone.

第四十章

论反复

　　林语堂说:"本章仅以短短的几句话,便总括了老子的学说。"这四句话是:"反者道之动,弱者道之用。天下万物生于有,有生于无。"总结起来,只有"反""弱""有""无"四个字。"反"是什么意思?林语堂解释第一句说:"道的运行本是反复循环的。"那么,"反"就是"反复循环"了。"道"是由弱到强,由强到弱,由有到无,由无到有,反复循环的吗?我们看看第二十五章关于"反"的解释:"吾不知其名,强字之曰道,强为之名曰大。大曰逝,逝曰远,远曰反。"英译文是:

> I do not know its name
> and call it the divine law
> or style it the great.
> What is great will circulate,
> What circulates will go a long way,
> and what goes a long way will return in the end.

第四十章　论反复

那就是说,老子不知道它叫什么名字,勉强叫它"道",或者是"大道",大道是循环往复的,循环往复的道路很长,再长的道路最后也要回到原处。为什么会回到原处呢?我们再看看第三十六章的解释:"将欲歙之,必固张之,将欲弱之,必固强之,将欲废之,必固兴之,将欲夺之,必固与之。"这就是说:如要收缩,先要扩张;如要削弱,先要加强;如要新兴,先要废旧;如要夺取,先要给予。这几句说明道的反复,可以翻译如下:

> Expansion before reduction, (Inhale before you exhale!)
> Strengthening before weakening, (Strengthen what is to be weakened!)
> Prosperity before decline, (Raise before its fall!)
> Giving before taking! (Give before you take!)

既然道是循环往复,一张一弛,时强时弱,有盛有衰,或取或予的,那就应该顺其自然,最好是先张后弛,先强后弱,先盛后衰,先予后取。因为自然顺序总是从无到有,从有到无的,从无到有就要先张,从有到无才能后弛,从无到有就要先强,从有到无才能后弱,盛衰,取予也是一样。还有一种解释,说天道可以有相反的道路:那就可以把"反者道之动"这一句译成:

> The divine law may go opposite ways.

这就是说:天道可开可合,可强可弱,可兴可废,可取可予。那也就是循环往复了。下面一句"弱者道之用"如何理解?我看老子主张以柔克刚,以弱胜强,所以这里可以理解为:软弱也有用处,可以用来战胜刚强。译成英文可以是:

> Even weakness is useful.

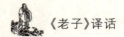《老子》译话

最后两句是:"天下万物生于有,有生于无。"这两句总结了前面几句的意思,如何理解更好?我个人认为"有"指"有形","无"指"无形",那就是说,"道"是无形的,根据无形的"道"产生了有形的万物,这就是"有生于无"。可以译成英文如下:

All things in the world come into being with a form, the form comes from the formless.

第四十一章

谈闻道

林语堂在《老子的智慧》第141页上说:"形成老子思想的哲学原理,完全包括在前四十章内,而后四十章处理的,大多是实际生活上的问题,比如生活的准则和政治论等。"第四十一章,他认为是谈道家特性的。开始时说:"上士闻道,勤而行之;中士闻道,若存若亡;下士闻道,大笑之,不笑之不足以为道。"这就是说,上等人闻道明理之后,会按照道理去做事;中等人听道之后,半信半疑,信的就会去做,不信的就不做了;下等人根本不信道,反而哈哈大笑。如果他不大笑,怎能知道他不信呢? 这几句可以翻译如下:

> Having heard the divine law, a good scholar follows it; a common scholar half believes in it; a poor scholar laughs at it. If not laughed at, it cannot be the divine law.

上士闻道,如何"勤而行之"呢? 比如说循环往复之道,先弱后强,然后先强后弱。一个人的成长总是由幼年到少年,少年到青年,青年到壮年,体力越来越强的;到了中年以后,体力开始衰退,到了老年,更加衰弱,这就是先强后弱了。一个闻道的人明白了由弱到强的道理,就要顺其自然,在青少年时期好好学习,充实自己,加强自己,到了由强转弱的时期,也要顺应自然,只做力所能及的事情,这是上士闻道而行之的做法。至于"勤而行之"呢,一个人的体力和脑力并不是相等的,中年之后,人的体力减弱了,智力并不一定减弱,那就还要尽其在我,这样才算"勤而行之"。"中士闻道,若存若亡",是说"道"似乎存在,又似乎不存在,那就是半信半疑了。就以"立国之道"为例,一个国家的成长发展,由小而大,从弱到强,是不是一定会盛极而衰呢?如果开始衰败,应该是顺其自然,还是应该力挽狂澜呢?这就是道家和儒家的分别了。道家主张让国家自然发展,儒家却主张知其不可为而为之。道家认为任其自然的是"上士",尽其在我的是"中士"。用今天的标准来衡量,到底道家或儒家是"上士"却是可以研究的了。而新中国成立前的中国一直受帝国主义的侵略压迫,不能说与道家的思想没有关系。至于"下士","下士闻道则大笑。"为什么会大笑呢?是笑上士还是笑中士?恐怕需要举例说明,而最好的例子可能是第二次世界大战的战败国日本。日本侵略中国,杀人无数,使中国受了巨大的损失。但中国实行了道家"予"而不"取"之道,没有要求日本赔偿。不料日本知道后哈哈大笑,反而变本加厉,强占中国领土钓鱼岛,拒不归还,另一方面,对二战后割让给俄国的北方四岛,却又妄称还是日本领土。像这样的霸权主义国家,你和他讲强弱取予之道,他听了只会哈哈大笑,他笑你强我弱的时候你不"取"而"予",现在我也强了,还有强者撑腰,怎能把原来属于你的领土归还给你?可见与下士之类的国家是不能讲道的。如果你给

第四十一章 谈闻道

他讲"取""予"之道,他认为你不要战争赔偿是理所当然,是合乎"予"之道的,那战败国不归还战前霸占的领土也是理所当然,是合乎"你予他取"之道的。如果你讲"以柔克刚"之道,他会认为那是长远的事,将来能否实现还不一定;而"以刚克柔"却是现实情况,正好强占你的领上,他不在乎将来由盛转衰,而只在乎现在由弱变强。所以对这种下等国家,不能谈道家之道,只能像西方人一样,以眼还眼,以牙还牙。

这样说来,谈道是不是要看对象,因人而异?上士信道,中士疑之,下士笑之。在我看来,上士太理想化,下士又太现实,还是中士既不太过,又非不及,颇得儒家中庸之道。但是老子谈道,主要是对上士,所以他接着说:"故建言有之:明道若昧,进道若退,夷道若类。"于是有人提出意见了,光明的大道看起来像黑暗的(或明白的道理听起来像是暧昧的),前进的道路像在倒退,平坦的大道显得崎岖不平。其实这三句话都是一个意思,就是括弧中的:明白的话听起来并不明白:如"以柔克刚""弱能胜强"。"柔弱"怎么能克服"刚强"呢?最常用的例子是"水滴石穿",柔软的水一滴一滴可以滴穿坚硬的石头,但这有个时间的问题,从长远的观点看来,水可以滴穿石头,但在短时间内,水是滴不穿石头的,所以刚柔相克是一个相对的道理。弱能胜强也是一样,如以解放战争为例。初期的国民党很强,有八百万人的军队;共产党比较弱,只有二百万人的军队,但是结果共产党打败了国民党,解放了全中国,这就证明了弱能胜强。不过这也有一方转弱为强,另一方转强为弱的过程,不能算是以弱胜强,还是弱转强后,战胜了强转弱的例子。总起来看,柔弱胜刚强是一个软实力可以胜过硬实力的问题,其次,为什么说前进的道路象倒退呢?以社会进步的道路为例,从按资

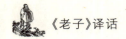《老子》译话

分配的资本主义到按劳分配的社会主义,走的是前进的道路,而从按劳分配的社会主义走向按需分配的共产主义,又更前进了一步。但共产主义道路和"大道之行也,天下为公"的原始共产主义却有相似之处,所以前进的道路看起来似乎是倒退了。其实这正说明了循环往复的道理。平坦的大道显得崎岖不平也是一样,因为"平"和"不平"是相对的,没有绝对的"平"。所以中国建设社会主义的道路也经历了反左反右,"文化大革命"的崎岖过程。因此,老子的话今天还有参考价值。这几句可译成英文如下:

> Therefore it is said the way to light seems dark; the forward way seems to go backward; the smooth way seems rough.

既然明暗进退,平坦崎岖都是相对的,于是老子进一步分析"德"说:"故上德若谷,广德若不足,建德若偷,质德若渝。"这就是说,高深的道德像低洼的山谷,广泛的德泽使人感觉不到,修养德行总觉得不够,朴实的德性却不显露出来。总而言之,就是虚怀若谷,用英文来说可以是:

> So high virtue looks like low vale, infinite virtue seems insufficient, established virtue seems borrowed, simplicity seems clumsy.

老子再把抽象的"德",用具体的事物来说明:"大白若辱,大方若隅,大器晚成,大音希声,大象无形。"洁白的东西看起来似乎也有污点,方方正正的东西却看不到棱角,伟大的事情总要等到最后才能完成,最大的声音是耳朵听不到的,最大的形象是眼睛看不见的。因为黑白方圆形声都是相对的,不可能达到绝对的程度,所以

第四十一章 谈闻道

要有自知之明。这些可以译成:

So purity seems soiled, a large square seems cornerless, a great vessel is the last completed, a great sound is inaudible, a great image is formless.

最后老子作结论说:"道隐无名,夫惟道善始且善成。"所以"道"也隐而不现,有实无名。只有"道"是始终如一的。译成英文可以是:

Only the divine law, invisible and nameless, is good from the beginning to the end.

第四十二章

正反合

　　第二十五章最后说:"人法地,地法天,天法道,道法自然。"这说出了"天人合一"之道。人如何能和天合一呢?第一,看地上的万物是如何生长发育的,然后进行耕种收割,这就是"人法地"。第二,地上的万物按照天道,春生夏长,秋结果,冬落叶,这可以说是"地法天"。第三,天让春夏秋冬四时运行,让万物自由生长发育,这就是"天法道"。第四,自然规律就是春暖夏热,秋凉冬寒,人的规律是生老病死,物的规律是成长消亡,"道"不过是顺其自然而已。这就是"道法自然"了。

　　到了这一章,老子进一步说:"道生一,一生二,二生三,三生万物。"例如"天人合一"之道,可以一分为二,分为"天""人";刚柔之道,可以分为"刚""柔";强弱之道,可以分为"强""弱"。这可以说是"一生二"。"天人合一"中的"天"是一,"人"是二,"天人合一"就是三。老子的以柔克刚之道,则"柔"是一,"刚"是二,刚柔结合,以柔克刚是三;以弱胜强之道也是一样,"弱"是一,"强"是二,"弱"

第四十二章 正反合

转为"强"是三。在我看来,一二三的关系正是辩证法的正反合的关系。这样现代化的解释就更能说明老子"三生万物"的道理了,因为万物都是按照"正反合"的规律发展进化的。因此,这几句话可以译成英文如下:

One is the child of the divine law, after one come two, after two come three, after three come all things.

老子接着说:"万物负阴而抱阳,冲气以为和。"这就说明了"正反合"的道理。"负"是"背负",是反面;"抱"是"怀抱",是正面。阴阳二气就代表刚柔两方面,强弱两方面,"冲气"就是阴气和阳气相结合,以柔克刚,以弱胜强,这就是"正反合"了。译成英文可以说是:

Everything has a bright (strong, hard) side and a dark (weak, sort) side, co-existent in harmony.

既然柔可克刚,弱能胜强,所以老子接着又说:"人之所恶惟孤寡不谷,而王公以为称。"人不喜欢孤寡,不在中心,因为孤寡柔弱,刚强才在中心,但是柔弱能胜刚强,所以王公自称"孤家""寡人",这就是"正反合"的一个例子。英文的意思是:

People dislike to be lonely and worthless, but the worthy rulers call themselves the sole and unworthy.

为什么呢?因为"物或损之而益,或益之而损。"损益是相对的,吃一堑,长一智,就是例子。所以王公自谦,反而可以赢得尊敬。用英文说则是:

So gain may turn into loss and loss into gain.

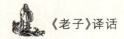《老子》译话

这种得失损益的相对的道理,是大家都知道的,最著名的例子是"塞翁失马,焉知祸福"的故事。所以老子说:"人之所教,我亦教之。"

  I will teach what I am taught.

最后,老子又从反面举了一个例子:"强梁者不得其死,吾将以为教父。"王公都是强者,但是如果谦虚,可以保住高位;如果逞强称霸,反而不得善终。这就是老子用相对论对强者敲响的警钟。

  The brute will die a brutal death. I will teach this as a lesson.

第四十三章

柔与刚

老子在上一章谈到柔可以克刚的道理,这一章又进一步做了发挥,并且提高成为抽象的理论。他接着说:"天下之至柔,驰骋天下之至坚。"这就是说,天下最柔软的东西,可以在天下最坚硬刚强的东西中自由行动。译成英文,"至柔"和"至坚"的五种译文大致相同,"驰骋"的译法却有五种:

> The softest thing in to world can penetrate (go through, run in and out of, control, overcome) the hardest.

五种译文大致可以还原译为:通过,跑进跑出,深入,克服,控制。到底哪种译文好呢?这要看对"至柔"和"至坚"的理解。在我看来,如果要用今天的话来解释,"至刚"是指物质,"至柔"则指精神。如果我的理解不错,那么,"通过"和"跑进跑出"虽然更接近原文"驰骋",但是不好理解,有所不足:"克服"和"控制"似乎又有过之。从今天的观点看来,精神恐怕既不能"克服",也不能"控制"物

《老子》译话

质,可能还是"深入"更合乎实际。尤其从下面一句"无有入无间"看来,说"一无所有"的精神可以进入"没有间隙"的物质,动词用的也是"入"字,可见"深入"的理解更好。译成英文又有几种:

1. There is no space but the matterless can enter.
2. What consists of no substance can enter what has no crevices.
3. The formless can enter where there is no space.
4. The invisible force penetrates any creviceless being.
5. The formless can penetrate anything that has no gaps.

"无有"的四种译文各有千秋,第二种译文用的是科学名词,第三、五种译文说是无形的,似乎不如第四种说"看不见的",总的说来,还是第一种用和"精神"对立的词汇更好。"无间"的第二、五种译文都好,第四种译文加入一个名词,可能容易引起误会。第一、三种都用"没有空间",但第一种说"没有精神进入不了的空间",第三种却说"无形的能进入没有空间的地方",那就不知所云了。

下面老子提升说:"吾是以知无为之有益。""无有"是指"无物"的客观状态,"无为"是指主观的无所作为。既然客观上说,精神可以进入物质,那么主观上人就可以任其自然,不要妨碍自然的发展,这就是有益的了。英文翻译也有几种,总起来说:

Thus I see (know) the utility (benefit, value, advantage) of doing nothing (inaction, taking no action, non-action).

"无为"是《老子》的关键词,翻译没有定论,甚至可以看具体情况,做具体翻译。这里如果译成 doing nothing wrong,可能更好理解。至于"有益"的四种译法各有千秋:"用处"和"价值"更客观,"利益"

第四十三章 柔与刚

和"好处"更主观。最后,老子作结论说:"不言之教,无为之益,天下希及之。"译成英文,就不再解释了。

The teaching by saying nothing(without words) and the utility of doing nothing are seldom known to the world.

第四十四章

得与失

老子说:"名与身孰亲?身与货孰多?得与亡孰病?"这里提出了三个问题:第一个问题是身体和名声的关系,哪一样对人更密切呢?答案一般是身体比名声对人的关系更密切,因为没有身体,名声就没有用处。但是"亲"也可以理解为"喜欢",一般人喜欢身体好,但也有人认为名誉重于生命的。第二个问题是身体和财物,哪一样的用处更多更大呢?这里身体是个必需条件,财物是个充分条件,也就是说,没有身体不行,但是只有身体也不一定有用;财物可以有用,但是没有财物也不是不行。一般说来,身体还是比财物更有用的。第三个问题是:得到和失掉,哪一样害处更大?一般人自然认为是"失掉"的害处大。但是这个问题的主观性更大,老子的看法就与人不同,下面就来看看两种英译文,第一种更客观,第二种更主观。

1. What is dearer (more precious), your name (fame) or your body (life)?

第四十四章 得与失

Which is more important (valuable), body (health) or goods (wealth)?

Which is more harmful (detrimental), gain or loss (your gains or losses, the gain of fame or the loss of health)?

2. Which do you love better, fame or life? Which do you like more, health or wealth? Which will do you more harm, gain or loss?

自然,主观和客观也是相对的,只是第一种译文问"孰亲?孰多?孰病?"仿佛问的是客观事实;而第二种译文问到爱好,喜欢,对你有害,却更像是征求主观的意见,所以我觉得第二种比第一种好一点。既然得失利害有主观的因素在内,那答案就可以因人而异了。

老子是怎样回答的呢?他说:"甚爱必大费,多藏必厚亡。"这就是说,如果你太爱你得到的东西,你必定会花费很多时间精力去保存,你保存得越多,将来失掉的也就越多。所以现在得到的东西或财物,失去的是时间和精力,得到的不一定比失掉的更多;而现在得到的东西,将来总是要失掉的(如你死后),所以算笔总账,得到的好处并不比失掉的好处更多。译成英文也可以有两种:

1. Excessive (unrestrained) stinginess (love of fame, covet for fame) will result in great expense (considerable costs); too much amassment (excessive hoarding, a rich hoard of wealth) leads (will give rise) to great (heavy) loss.

2. The more you love, the more you spend. The more you store up, the more you lose.

第一种译文把"爱"理解为贪财爱名,把"藏"理解为储藏财物;第二

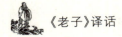

种范围更广,应用的范围也就更大。老子是怎样回答的呢?他说,"故知足不辱,知止不殆,可以长久"。结论是:知足才可以不自取其辱,适可而止才可以不冒风险,这样才能维持长久。结论并不限于财物,但是可以包括财物,这样看来,译文还是第二种好一些。因此结论可以译成:

As a result, contentment brings no shame; knowledge of the limit brings no danger. Thus you can be safe for long.

第四十五章

论大成

上一章谈到身名利失的矛盾统一,这一章接着谈成败,盈虚,曲直,技拙等的辩证关系。开始时说:"大成若缺,其用不弊。"意思就是:大功告成并不是没有缺点,但是作用可以维持长久不衰。译成英文就是:

Perfection does not seem flawless, but it can be used for long.

但是 perfection(完美)之前有人加了 complete(完全的),有人加了 most(最大,最多),似乎没有必要,因为"完美"已经是最高级了。"不弊"有人说 its use cannot be exhausted(无穷无尽)或 inexhaustible(不可穷尽),倒也精确。

第二句说:"大盈若冲,其用不穷。"意思也是:装得满满的看起来却像是空空的,但是用起来却永远也用不完。可以翻译如下:

What is full still has vacancy, but it can be used endlessly.

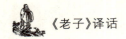

"若冲"到底是"好像是空的"还是"其中有空隙"呢？从字面上看是前者，从逻辑上看却可能是后者。不过无论前后，结论都是一样的。

接着又提出了三种辩证关系："大直若屈，大巧若拙，大辩若讷"。这三种关系似乎前者是内容，后者是方法或形式。这就是说，内容正直，方法却要婉转曲折，内容巧妙，形式却并不妙语惊人；辩才无碍，讲起来也并不口若悬河，反而慢吞吞的字斟句琢，总要十拿九稳才肯出口；这三句可以译成如下英文：

The straight may seem crooked, the most skillful may seem clumsy, the most eloquent may seem slow of speech.

"大巧""大辩"的译文都用了最高级的形容词 most，"大直"也有人译成 straightest 或 most straight，但英文物质的"直"没有比较级和最高级；"屈"字译成 bent 表示弯曲一次，crooked 却是弯弯曲曲。"拙"字译成 clumsy 是客观的描写，awkward 带有主观的看法，"讷"字译成 tongue-tied（张口结舌）就比结结巴巴还更严重，简直说不出话来了；有人译成 mute，更有"余欲无言"的哲学意味。

最后的结论是："静胜躁，寒胜热，清静为天下正。"这又提出了动和静，寒和热的矛盾。老子主张以静制动，以柔克刚，以寒胜热，所以认为天下的正道是清静无为，这是老子的基本思想。译文有两种：

1. The tranquil overcomes the hasty; the cold overcomes the heat. By remaining quiet and tranquil, one can be a model for all the people.

2. Be calm rather than rash, be cool rather than hot,

第四十五章 论大成

Serenity is the right way in the world.

第一种译文是客观的描述,说只要清静就可以成为人民的榜样。第二种是主观的要求,要冷静而不要躁动,因为清静是人们的正道。还有版本说"躁胜寒,静胜热",这里就不讨论了。

第四十六章

论知足

　　这一章先谈有道无道的分别:"天下有道,却走马以粪,天下无道,戎马生于郊。"说是如果治理天下,都能按照道理进行,那么,战争用的军马,可以用来拉车运粪,施肥产粮。如果治理天下不能按照道理进行,那么耕田用的母马也要用作战马,甚至会在战场上生下小马来。这就用具体的事例说明了抽象的道理。但是"道"字如何翻译呢?一种译音,译成 Tao 或 Dao;一种译意译为 Way,way 或 law。译音毫无意义,译者自己未必了解,读者更是莫明其妙,翻译等于不译,不如译意,根据具体情况,译出具体的意义。这两句话可以有不同的译文:

　　1. When the Tao (or Dao) prevails in the world, the battle steeds (or war horses) are returned to farmers for tilling (ploughing) the fields; when the Tao does not prevail (or is absent) in the world, even pregnant mares are taken over for wars (have to serve in battle or colts are bred on the fields).

第四十六章 论知足

2. When the Way is implemented in the world, the battle steeds will be returned to the farmers to carry manures. When the Way is not implemented in the world, the mares will be forced to the battlefields and give birth to foals there.

3. When the world goes the right way, battle steeds are used for tillage. When the world goes the wrong way, pregnant mares are used in war.

比较一下几种译文,可以说"道"的第一种译文不如第二种,而第二种"有道"的译文又不如第一种,因为它把"道"当作推行的工具,而不是按照"道"去行事,所以还是第三种译文最好,"走马以粪"的第二种译文说"用马运粪",最为精确,但运粪只是手段,目的却是肥田耕种,所以只译耕种地也就够了。第三种译文又比第一种精炼。"无道"的译文也是一样。第二种译文说雌马被迫当战马用,自然不错,但说"戎马生于郊"也是被迫的,又显得牵强了,所以翻译需要具体情况分析。有些大同小异的译文可以仁者见仁,智者见智。

上面举的是具体的事例,下面上升为抽象的理论:"祸莫大于不知足;咎莫大于欲得。"不知足是从反面说,贪得是从正面说的,说天下有道,人就应该知足,而不知足是最大的坏事,最大的错误是贪得无厌,最后的结论是:"故知足之足,常足矣。"只要你知道"知足"是"足"是什么意思,你就永远会有足够了的。这几句话可以翻译如下:

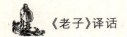《老子》译话

No crime is greater than insatiable desire(greediness); no woe is greater than covetise (discontent). If you know contentment comes from being content, you will always have enough.

第四十七章

论天道

　　这是老子谈论天道的一章,有各种各样的解释。我只能根据自己的理解来翻译。一开始说:"不出户,知天下,不窥牖,见天道。""天下"是什么意思?是天下的事情,还是天下的人心?"天道"如何理解?前面已经谈过,现在先来看看几种译文:

　　1. Without going out of the door (stirring out of the house, or stepping outside your door) one can know (see) everything (what is happening) in the world (under heaven); without looking out of the window, one can (may) see (understand) the Tao (law) of heaven.

　　2. You may know the outside world without going out; you may know the divine law without looking out of the window.

"不出户"的译文大同小异,第二种译文没有译"户"字,但并没有改变原意,比较简练,"知天下"的第一种译文说是天下的各种事物或发生的事情,说得太具体了,是不是符

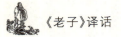《老子》译话

合老子的原意？可以研究。第二种译文只说"外部世界",世界包括地、物、人,也包括人的思想心理在内。一个人不必出门,就可以了解外部世界人的思想心理,这是可以想象得到的,但是不出门能不能知道天下的万事万物,或世界上的一切事情呢？老子那时还没有报纸或电讯,可能性恐怕不大。所以从今天的观点看来,第二种译文使老子更近情理。至于"天道"的译文,音译不能使读者有所了解；意译第一种更接近自然规律,第二种更抽象,合乎天人合一的思想。

下面接着说:"其出弥远,其知弥少。"说是出门走得越远,知道的反而越少,这句的翻译几乎没有什么不同,大致都是：

> The farther you go out, the less you may learn.

但是如何解释呢？如果把"知天下"理解为天下的事物,那应该是走得越远,知道的事情越多才对。如果把天下理解为天下人的心理,那么不必出门,只要将心比心,就可推己及人,了解天下的人心了。如果走得太远,知道的人太多,而人心又不同,不一定能推己及人,那了解就反而少了,由此可见理解的重要。

最后的结论是:"是以圣人不行而知,不见而名,无为而成。"根据上下文来看,"不行而知"应该是说：不必远行就可以知道世界。"不见"是不是指"不窥牖",或是不表现自己反而能成名呢？最后的"无为而成"应该是"无为而无不为",有所不为才能有所为,才能有所成；不做错事,不乱干涉,才能使人各尽所能,各有所成。这几句可译成英文如下：

> Therefore the sage learns all without going far away, he becomes wellknown without looking for fame, and accomplishes all without doing anything wrong.

第四十八章

论损益

第一章谈"道"与"学"的矛盾:"为学日益,为道日损。"说得到知识一天比一天多,懂得道理(需要的知识)却一天比一天少。为什么呢?解释又有各种各样。我们先看看不同的翻译:

1. He who seeks learning must increase his knowledge everyday; he who seeks the Tao must reduce his knowledge everyday.

2. He who pursues knowledge learns more day by day; he who pursues Tao does less day by day.

3. The pursuit of learning is to increase day after day; the pursuit of the Dao is to decrease day after day.

4. As to seeking knowledge, the desire should increase with each passing day; as to seeking the Way, the desire should decrease with each passing day.

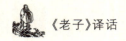

5. The more you know of the human world, the less you know of the divine law.

第一种译文说：求学必须每日增加知识，求"道"必须每日减少知识。第二种说：求知天天学得多，求"道"天天做得少。第三种说：求知一天天增加，求"道"一天天减少。第四种说：求知时欲望应该逐日增加，求道时欲望应该逐日减少。第五种说：对人世的知识越多，对天道的了解就越少。五种译文都有道理，到底谁是谁非？或者并无是非，只好仁者见仁，智者见智了，可见老子的思想可以广泛并用，不过五种译文的共同点是求知不能忘"道"，不能本末倒置。

下面接着说："损之又损，以至于无为。"这就可以理解为：求"道"可以损失知识，损失直到无所作为而止。译文选了三种：

2. Less and less is done until nothing is done at all.

4. It is finally reduced to the state of "non-action".

5. Less and less you need to know till nothing need to be done.

"无为"是什么意思呢？下面补充说："无为而无不为。"意思就是说：有所不为，也有所为，有所不为是错误的事，妨碍别人自由的事；有所为的是正确的事，是让人各尽所能的事。这是老子"无为"的真正意义。译文只有一种说得过去：

When you need do nothing wrong, there is nothing you cannot do.

这就是说，如果你不是被动，而是主动去做需要你做的事，那就没有什么事不能够做。最后把个人的事扩大到天下事说："取天下常

第四十八章　论损益

以无事,及其有事,不足以取天下。"意思就是:天下可以无为而治。如果干涉别人自由,使人不能各尽所能,那就做不好天下事了。总之,无为指为私,有为指为公,结论可以译成英文如下:

If you need do nothing wrong, you can rule over the world. If everything need you to do, you cannot rule over the world.

第四十九章

论常心

"无为而治",上一章讲了无为而无不为,就是有所不为,才能有所作为。这一章再讲无为是"无常心":"圣人无常心,以百姓心为心。""常心"是什么?有两种解释:一种说是经常的,一成不变的心理;另一种说是"成见",是"私心"。第一种的范围更广,包括第二种在内;第二种更具体,更容易理解。全句说:"圣人治理天下,没有一成不变的成规陋矩,没有成见,没有私心,而是深入了解民心,老百姓怎么想,自己就怎么想。译成英文就是:

The sage has no personal will, he takes the people's will as his own.

下面接着解释:"善者吾善之,不善者吾亦善之,德善。"这就是说,老百姓对我好,我也对他们好;即使对我不好的人,我对他们也一样好。这样,老百姓都好起来了,"德善"就是"得善",善有善报,这是老子的理想主义,可以译成英文如下:

He is good not only to those who are good, but also to those who are not, so all become good.

第四十九章 论常心

同样的道理,"信者吾信之,不信者吾亦信之,德信。"意思还是:老百姓相信我,我也相信他们;即使不相信我的人,我也一样相信。这样,大家都得到了信任,彼此就互相信任。这句可以翻译如下:

> He trusts not only the trustworthy, but also those who are not, so all become trustworthy.

"无为而治"就是没有成见,没有私心,这样治理天下,就能和老百姓和好相处,互相信任,人人都能尽其在我,发挥最大的主观能动性,这就是无为而无不为,无私而天下大治。而圣人呢,"圣人在天下,歙歙焉,为天下浑其心。""歙歙"是"收敛"的意思,"浑"是"浑然纯朴"的意思,就是说领导人并不居功自大,而是和老百姓一样单纯相素,各尽所能,那就天下太平了,这有几种译文:

> 1. The sage lives (governs, is amiable) in the world, diligently uniting the hearts of the people (help everyone return to the sphere of simplicity, appear to be slow-witted).
>
> 2. The sage seems simple in the world; he simplifies all the people's mind.

"歙歙"可以说是"单纯",说是"和蔼可亲"带有褒义。"浑"字译成"团结"比较现代化。不如"单纯化"和"歙歙"一致,"迟钝"却有贬义,所以感觉得第二种译文好些。最后两句是:"百姓皆注其耳目,圣人皆孩之。"说老百姓都注意听圣人的话,圣人使他们像孩子一样纯洁了。结句可以译成:

> The people are all eyes and ears; the sage restores them to their childhood.

第五十章

论生死

圣人使百姓有赤子之心,可以常葆青春,这是养生之道。因为"出生入死,生之徒十有三,死之徒十有三,人之生,动之于死地,亦十有三。"这话有不同的解释。一种说是从生到死,活得长寿的有十分之三,知命而死的也有十分之三,还有三分之一处在生死之间,或者死亡边缘,译成英文就是:

> From birth to death, one-third of men live long, one-third die early, and one-third die from their own choice though they could have lived longer. (strive for long life but meet with premature or unnatural death, or live and move near the realm of death or at death's door).

后半句的第一种译文说自愿早死,第二种说是非自然死亡,第三种只说是在死亡门外。这些说法都显得牵强。另一种解释是:在生死搏斗中,三分之一能活下来,三分之一死去,三分之一在生死之间,这个解释更近情理,可

第五十章 论生死

以译成英文如下:

> In the life-and-death struggle, one-third of men may live, one-third may die, and one-third will be in the realm between life and death.

下面接着问道:"夫何故?以其生生之厚。"为什么呢?因为应该重视生命。这个问题可以翻译如下:

> How can it be so? For men should value a long life.

如何重视生命呢?回答是具体的例子:"盖闻善摄生者,陆行不遇兕虎,入军不被甲兵;"一个爱惜生命的人,在陆地上不会走到老虎和犀牛出没有地方去,打仗的时候也会躲避全副武装的士兵。结果呢?"兕无所投其角,虎无所措其爪,兵无所容其刃。"这就是说,不要让犀牛的角碰到,不要让老虎的爪子抓住,不要让士兵的刀枪伤害。这就是看重生命的例子,也是看重生命的方法,意思是说,不要轻举妄动,去冒不必要的危险。译文大致如下:

> In fact, those who value (or are good at preserving) their life will not go near rhinos or tigers on land, nor go to war in armor or shield so that rhinos have no use of their horns and tigers of their claws and soldiers of their swords.

结论是:"夫何故?以其无死地。"为什么没有危险呢?因为他们不会到危险的地方去。最后一句的"死地"有几种译文:

1. Because there is no realm of death for him to enter.
2. Because death has nowhere to enter.
3. Because there is no place in his body that is fatal.

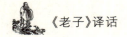《老子》译话

4. For they will not come near the realm of death.

为什么没有死地,为什么身体没有致命的弱点?前三种译文知其然而不知其所以然,只有第四种说不冒危险,合乎情理。

第五十一章

论道德

这一章"道德"并提:"道生之,德蓄之。""道"是道理,"德"是品德,全句是说:万物都按道理生长,"德"就是"得",万物按照道理生长,得到了一种品德,或者说物之所以为物的德性、本质。万物的本质经过培养就会发展,变得更加完善。译成英文可以是:

Everything grows in accordance with the divine law; it is bred in its internal virtue.

这里"德"指万物内在的品德,接着说:"物形之,势成之。"这里的"物"指一物之外的万物,指形成一物的外在物质环境,"势"指外在物质对形成物的影响。总之,一物的形成既有内因,也有外因,既有具体的"形",也有抽象的"势",可见老子的思想符合今天的辩证唯物主义,这句可以译成英文如下:

It is formed by its environment and completed by external influence.

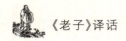《老子》译话

结果就是:"是以万物莫不尊道而贵德。""尊敬"的意义广泛,可以有不同的译文:

> That is why all things(creatures)obey(worship, respect or venerate)the divine law (Tao, the Way)and value (honor or treasure)their own virtue.

"道"有音译意译,"德"的译文却都一样,"物"也大同小异,只有一种译成 creatures,那就限于生物,"尊"译 worship(崇拜),venerate (尊崇)都太重,respect(尊重)比较抽象,obey(遵从)比较具体。"敬"译 honor(尊敬)抽象,treasure(珍视)略重,value(认为有价值)更具体,可能合适一点。接着又强调说:"道之尊,德之贵,夫莫之命,而常自然。"万物尊道贵德是自然现象,不是遵从命令。译为"道"是无所不能的,"德"是有价值的,全句译文就是:

> The divine law is omnipotent and virtue is valuable. None orders them to be obeyed, but they are obeyed naturally.

接着更进一步展开来说:"故道生之,德蓄之,长之育之,成之熟之,养之复之。"因此万物按照道理生长,培养自己的品德,发育成熟,无处不在"道"的覆盖之下,译文和前面的大同小异。

> In accordance with the divine law all things are born and bred in their virtue, grown up and developed, completed and matured, protected and sheltered.

最后又从反面来说:"生而不有,为而不恃,长而不宰,是谓玄德。""道"使万物生长,并不占有万物,使万物有所为,并不自恃有功;

第五十一章　论道德

"道"引领万物,却不主宰,这就是道德玄妙的地方。可以翻译如下:

Creation without possession, action without supervision, leadership without domination, such is the mystery of virtue.

第五十二章

论习常

第一章有各种解释,一开始说:"天下有始,以为天下母。""天下"可能是指万物,万物有始。四十二章说了:"道生一,一生二,二生三,三生万物。"万物始于一,而一生于"道",所以"道"就是"天下母",译成英文就是:

> The world has beginning regarded as its mother.

后面接着说:"既得其母,以知其子。"意思就是:既然知道了万物产生的道理,那就可以根据道理来了解万物。译文却只能是:

> If you know the mother, you can know her sons.

下面又接着说:"既知其子,复守其母,没身不殆。"既然了解天下万物,又能按照道理做事,那你一生都不会犯错误,不会冒危险了。翻译却可以只翻宣示义,不翻启示义:

第五十二章 论习常

　　If you know the sons and still follow the mother, you may do nothing wrong(avoid danger)all your life long.

上半段打比喻，下半段推论说："塞其兑，闭其门，终身不勤。"既懂得抽象的道理，又能应用于具体的事物，那就不会犯错误了。"兑"字和"悦"字通用，指抽象的喜悦，七情六欲，"门"指具体的感官门户，眼耳口鼻等五官四肢，懂得道理就要应用，就要闭眼塞耳，不追求欲望的满足，那就可以终身不劳累，不痛苦。译文如下：

　　Dull your senses and shut their doors, you deed not toil all your life.

反过来说："开其兑，济其事，终身不救。"如果放纵你的感官，满足你的欲望，享受你的声色犬马之乐，那你这一生就不可救药了。这句可以翻译如下：

　　Awake your senses and satisfy your desires, you will be incurable all your life.

为什么这样说呢？因为"见小曰明，守柔曰强。"事无论大小，都要看清楚，不仅是大事，小事也一样，要小中见大，才能算聪明。人有刚强柔弱，但是强不一定胜弱，柔却可以克刚，软实力有时比硬实力更有用，柔和反而可以成为坚强，这种眼力心力可以译为：

　　Keen sight can see the smallest thing; supple mind can resist the strongest force.

最后一段太好懂。"用其光，复归其明，无遗身殃，是为习常。"用什么光？大约是在"道"的光辉照耀下，"复归其明"，大约是恢复明察秋毫的智慧。"无遗身殃"大约是不要让身体遭殃。"是为习

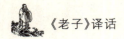

常用"大约是应该常做的事情,有人说是"常道",但不能肯定,只好勉强翻译如下:

Make, use of light to restore keen sight without endangering yourself. Let this be your habitual practice.

第五十三章

论大道

上一章讲欲望不能放任自流,这一章从反面讲放纵私欲的害处,开始时说:"使我介然有知,行于大道,惟施是畏。"这一句有不同的解释,一种认为:如果对"道"有点了解,就要跟着"道"走,只怕走错了路,另一种:"道"要顺其自然,不能有所为而为。译成英文,可能前者更好理解:

Little as know, I will follow the great Way, only afraid to go astray.

下面接着讲:"大道甚夷,而民好径。""险夷"是对立的,"甚夷"就是没有危险,大道和大路一样平坦而平安,但人却喜欢走小路。

The great Way is even, but people may like the by-path.

人们不走大道,而走小径,结果怎么样呢?"朝甚除,田甚芜,仓甚虚。""朝"指进行朝廷,"除"有两种解释:一说

"除"是整齐清洁,朝廷搜刮钱财,修整宫廷,而百姓穷苦,民不聊生。另一说"朝甚除者,谓朝廷尚施为,要贿赂,去君子,取小人,甚开私小之路也。"这就是说朝廷腐败的意思。前者说腐败的原因,后者说腐败的结果,译成朝廷腐败,田园荒芜,仓库空虚,也就行了,所以译文是:

  If the court is corrupt, the fields will be waste and the granaries empty.

田园仓库说的是民间的事,而朝廷的达官贵人呢?"服文采,带利剑,厌饮食。"那就是说,达官贵人都穿着华丽的衣服,佩带锋利的宝剑,丰富的酒肉都吃厌腻了,译成英文就是:

  But the lords are magnificently dressed, carrying precious sword and satiated with food and drink.

这样贫富对比,就可以看出大道和小路的分别了,于是结论是:"财货有余,是为盗竽,非道也哉。"有些版本的标点不同,把"财货有余"归入上句,那就是说贪官丰衣足食,享受着奢侈的物质生活。放在下句,却是总结达官贵人的"富",和上文平民百姓的"贫"形成鲜明对比。还有一种解释,认为"服文采"等几句的主语不是官而是民,这种说法比较牵强,就不加讨论了。"盗竽"的"竽"是一种乐器,奏乐的时候先吹竽,所以竽是领先的乐器,"盗竽"就是盗窃领导地位,这里等于说:盗窃财货都是歪门邪道,都是小径,距离大道有十万八千里,译成英文可有放前放后两种:

  1. If lords are magnificently dressed, carrying precious sword, satiated with food and drink, and possessed of fabulous wealth, they may be called thieves and robbers not going the

right way.

2. Possessed of fabulous fortune, they may be called chiefs of thieves, far from the right way.

第五十四章

论修道

第五十一章讲道德,第五十二三章讲道,这一章讲修德,先从反面讲"修","善建者不拔,善抱者不脱。"说会修建的人,建筑不会连根拔掉,会拥抱的人,拥抱的东西不会脱离怀抱。宋代范应元注释说:"善建德者,深而不拔,善抱德者,因而不脱。"这就是说,建设道德,要深入人心,不容易拔掉;怀抱道德,要固守不放松,身体力行,不能脱离实践.译成英文就是:

What is well-established cannot be rooted up; what is tightly held will not slip away.

这是抽象说理,如何具体应用呢?下面举了一个实例:"子孙以祭祀不辍。"如果善于修德,那么子孙就会感恩戴德,不断祭祀祖先。

What is worshiped by descendants will continue to exist.

于是言归正传,谈到修德了。"修之于身,其德乃真。"说

第五十四章 论修道

如果能身体力行,那才能算真正有"德",译成英文就是:

> Cultivated in the person, the virtue is true.

修身,齐家,治国,平天下,是一步一步来做的,所以下面就由身而家,由家而乡,由乡而国,由国而天下了。"修之于家,其德乃余;修之于乡,其德乃长;修之于国,其德乃丰;修之于天下,其德乃普。"如果一个家庭能修德行善,那么积善之家就会庆有余;如果一乡都能修德,那德行就会源远流长;如果一国能够以德为本,那国家就会物质精神双丰收;如果普天下都重德轻利,那就是大道之行也,天下为公了。这一段可以翻译如下:

> Cultivated in the family, it (virtue) will be plentiful; cultivated in the country, it will be durable; cultivated in the state, it will be abundant; cultivated in the world, it will be universal.

于是得出结论:"故以身观身,以家观家,以乡观乡,以国观国,以天下观天下。""以身观身"就是将心比心,推己及人,己所不欲,勿施于人,家国天下也是一样,观察自己的家庭、乡里、国家,就可以了解其他家庭、乡里、国家;根据自己所了解的天下,也可以推论出自己所不知道的天下。还有一种解释说:要用修身,齐家,治国,平天下之道来观照个人、家乡、国家、天下。译文则可以是:

> So judge another man by yourself, another family by your family, another country by your country, another state by your state, and the world unknown by the world you know (in the Way of cultivating personal moral character, regulating families, living together in peace and unity, governing the

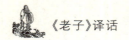

state, making peace).

最后,"吾何以知天下然哉?以此。"老子怎么知道天下是怎样的?就是用这种方法,译成英文就是:

How can I know about the world? Just in this way.

第五十五章

论厚德

上一章谈修德,这一章谈厚德,并且把厚德比作婴儿:"含德之厚,比之赤子。""含德"就是内心的德性,"厚"是充实的意思。内心包含的德性越充实,外在的表现就越自然,没有做作的姿态,就像婴儿的表现一样,译成英文就是:

A man of high virtue may be compared to a new-born baby.

婴儿的表现怎么样呢?"毒虫不螫,猛兽不据。"毒虫不会咬婴儿,猛兽也不会把婴儿当作食物,据为己有。还有一种解释是:毒虫不会咬自己的幼虫,猛兽也不会伤害自己的后代,后者更好翻译。

Poisonous insects will not sting their young, nor will fierce beasts bite theirs.

但从上下文的联系看来,却是前者更好解释,因为下面接着说:"骨弱筋柔而握固。"说婴儿的筋骨柔弱,但是手的

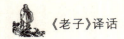《老子》译话

握力还好，抓住东西不放，说明还是抓得牢固的。这句可以译成英文如下：

> The young have weak bones and supple muscles, but their grasp is firm.

接着又说："未知牝牡之合而朘作，精之至也。"这也是说婴儿不知道男女公母结合的事，但是还有性感，因为这是人的本能。译成英文就是：

> They know nothing about sex, but their organ can be stirred, for they have instinct.

下面还是说婴儿："终日嚎而不嗄，和之至也。"婴儿一天到晚啼哭，但是声音不会嘶哑，因为这是符合自然的。这句可以译成：

> They cry all day without becoming hoarse because their cry conforms to nature.

厚德就要符合自然。所以接着又说："知和曰常，知常曰明。"知道一切要合乎自然，行动就会合乎规律；知道自然规律就是聪明。这个理论的译文是：

> Knowing nature, one will be constant in action; constant in action, one will be wise.

后面更发挥说："益生曰祥，心使气曰强。"这句有不同的解释，从字面看，可以理解为：有益于身体或生命的就是吉祥的，精力充沛就是强壮的。另外一种解释把"祥"和"强"都看成贬义词，我看有点牵强，不如按字面译成：

> A body full of life is good; a mind full of vigor is strong.

第五十五章 论厚德

最后再从正面谈到反面:"物壮则老,谓之不道,不道早已"这就是物极必反,由盛而衰的道理,是符合自然规律的。译文如下:

Anything past its prime will decline. If you think it not in the right way, you would be wrong.

第五十六章

论玄同

上一章谈了自然规律和处世之道,这一章谈社会规律。"知者不言,言者不知。"知道的人不一定说出来,说出来的人不一定知道,这讲的是知和言的矛盾。还有一种解释是:懂得天道的人不谈天道,谈天道的人往往不懂得天道。译成英文可有几种:

1. Those who know may (do) not speak; those who speak may (do) not know.

2. The wise person is of few words and the talkative person is not wise.

3. Those who know the divine law will not talk about it, and those who talk about it may not know it.

为什么"知者不言"?因为知道什么就说什么,似乎是在表现自己。而社会习惯是不喜欢表现自己的人,因为表现自己,往往显得小看了别人,所以下面接着说,"塞其兑,闭其门,挫其锐,解其纷;和其光,同其尘;是为玄同。"

第五十六章 论玄同

"兑"就是"悦",指喜怒哀乐,七情六欲。"塞其兑"就是要堵塞自己的欲望,"闭其门"是要关闭感官的门户,"挫其锐"是要挫折自己的锐气,不要锋芒外露;"解其纷"是要解决纠纷,"和其光"是不要光辉照耀得刺人眼目,"同其尘"是要把自己看得等同于尘世的普通人。"是为玄同。"这才是和玄妙的天道合而为一了。这段可以译成英文如下:

> Dull (curb) your senses (block the organs of desire) and shut your door (guard the door to your heart); blunt the sharp and solve the dispute (untangle your knots, free from troubles); soften the light (conceal your brilliance) and mingle with the dust (mix with the worldly people or be as humble as dust) so as to be one with the mysterious law (This is known as mystical union with virtue).

"玄同"的结果呢?"故不可得而亲,不可得而疏;不可得而利,不可得而害;不可得而贵,不可得而贱,故为天下贵。"这样,天下人和万物一样,没有亲疏贵贱之分,天下事也无所谓利害得失之别。因为人和天道(自然)合而为一了,而根据天道,自然界的万物是没有亲疏贵贱,利害得失的。天下很难找到这种"玄同"(天人合一)的人,所以是可贵的。这个结论可以译成两种英文:

> 1. (Since you are one with nature,) none could be your friend or foe; none could do you good or harm, none could honor or dishonor you. It is difficult to find such a man in the world.

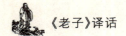

2. The sage is not moved by affection or disaffection, by gain or loss, by honor or disgrace; therefore, he is honored by all under heaven.

第五十七章

治国论

修身要按天道，治国也要按天道（或正道）。"以正治国，以奇用兵，以无事取天下。"大道并不是一成不变的，而是要根据具体情况具体分析。如治国要根据公正的道理，因为国人是国内的人民，是内部的问题，所以要按正道；而战争是对外部敌人的，那就需要出奇制胜，要按奇道，至于治天下呢，那却需要正反两手并用，不能用错，"无为而治"就是治国不能做错事，不能干涉人的自由。译成英文就是：

Rule tile state in an ordinary way, but fight the war in an extra-ordinary way. Win the world by doing nothing wrong.

下面问为什么？"吾何以知其然哉？以此：天下多忌讳，而民弥贫；民多利器，国家滋昏；人多技巧，奇物滋起；法令滋彰，盗贼多有。"我怎么知道应该这样做呢？因为干涉越多，禁止做的事越多。百姓就越贫困；老百姓的武器越多，国家就越混乱；人越重视技巧，欺骗讹诈的事就出来了；法律条条框框越多，盗贼也就越多，这就是道高一

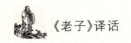《老子》译话

尺,魔高一丈的道理。用英文来说是:

> How can I know this is right? For the following reasons: more prohibitions in the world will impoverish people; more armed people will bring trouble to the state; the more shrewd people are, the more tricks will they do; the more laws and decrees are proclaimed, the more outlaws will appear.

于是结论就是:"故圣人云:我无为而民自化;我好静而民自正;我无事而民自富;我无欲而民自朴。"所以圣人说:只要自己不做错事,老百姓自然会走上正路,规规矩矩,老老实实做人;只要自己甘心情愿过平静恬淡的和平生活,百姓自然不会喜欢战争;只要自己不干涉百姓的自由,百姓自然会尽自己的本分;只要自己不损人利己,百姓自然会过上富足的生活;只要自己不贪图非分,百姓自然会老实朴素。总而言之,就是要以身作则,做好榜样,百姓自然会奉公守法。译文大同小异,现在总结归纳如下:

> 1. Therefore, the sage says: if I do nothing wrong, the people will go the right way; if I love peace, the people will not go to war; if I do not impoverish them, they will become rich; if I have no selfish desire, they will naturally be simple.
>
> 2. I take no action and people become honest (transformed, educated); I enjoy quietness (love tranquility) and people become peaceful (righteous); I meddle (disturb, intervene) not in busy affairs and people become rich (prosperous); I have no desires (are not greedy) and people become simple and good (honest).

第五十八章

论祸福

上一章说:"以正治国。"第一章说:"其政闷闷,其民淳淳。"政者正也,从政就是治国,就是要行正道,正道就是要扪心自问:是不是对百姓有好处?如果有,百姓自然会走上正道,纯朴做人。接着从反面说:"其政察察,其民缺缺。"如果治国似乎明察秋毫,事无巨细,都要苛刻求全,使老百姓爽然若失,不知所措,这就不是正道了,这两句有几种不同的英译文:

> If the government is lenient (magnanimous, generous and non-discriminary, fatuous and debauched), the people will be simple (honest and sincere, pure). If the government is severe (harsh, incorruptible and upright), the people will feel a lack of freedom (become cunning, crafty, troublesome).

"闷闷"和"察察"不大好译,理解也不相同,有正有反,有粗有细。如以对比而论,那么,lenient(宽松)和severe(严格)比较合适;generous(慷慨)褒义略多,non-discriminary

（无歧视的）无褒无贬，magnanimous（慷慨大方）褒义更重，fatuous（荒唐）和 debauched（堕落）却又贬义太重。"察察"译成 harsh（粗暴）带有贬义，译成 incorruptible（不会腐败的）和 upright（正直的）褒义稍重。"淳淳"几种译文大同小异；"缺缺"译为 lack of freedom（缺少自由）比较恰当，crafty（有技巧），cunning（狡猾），troublesome（麻烦）多少带有贬义，这是理解的不同，很难说谁是谁非。

下面的结论是："祸兮福之所倚；福兮祸之所伏。"灾祸和苦难的磨炼使人聪明能干，这是因祸得福；成功的喜悦使人得意忘形，可能招致失败，这又是福中隐藏着祸根。这两句话可以翻译如下：

Weal comes after woe; woe lies under weal.

译文说是祸去福来；福中有祸，祸中有福，说明了祸福的内外先后关系。接着又问："孰知其极？"谁知道祸福有没有极端，有没有无祸的福，无福的祸呢？回答说："其无正也，正复为奇，善复为妖。人之迷，其日固久。""正"和"奇"就是正反面，正面会变成后面，正如善会变成恶一样，这个问题使人迷惑，已经很长久了。"是以圣人方而不割，廉而不刿，直而不肆，光而不耀。"所以有道的圣人自己方正，但不伤人；自己廉洁，但不苛求别人；自己正直而不放肆，光明而不耀眼。这一段话可以翻译如下：

Who knows the line of demarcation? There is no absolute norm. The normal may turn into the abnormal; the good may turn into evil. People are perplexed at this for a long time. Therefore, the sage is fair and square without a cutting edge, thrifty but not exacting, straightforward but not haughty, bright but not dazzling.

第五十九章

论积德

治国先要治人。"治人事天,莫如啬。"治人是为了替天行道,而替天行道,最重要的是节俭。为什么呢?"夫惟啬,是为早服。"因为只有节省力量,才能早早做好准备。这几句话有不同的理解。也有不同的翻译:

1. To rule people and serve Heaven, nothing is better than frugality (restraint in action). Only by frugality can one conform early to the divine law.

2. The best way to govern the state and keep in good health is to stint vitality (to be sparing with one's energy). To stint vitality means an attempt in early preparation (to get ready early, in advance).

"啬"可以理解为减少行动,也可以理解为节省精力。"早服"则可以是早合天道,或者早做准备,为什么呢?接着的解释是:"早服谓之重积德。""早服"就是看重积德,译文可有两种:

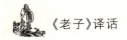

1. Early conformity means accumulation of virtue.

2. In making preparations in advance, he is accumulating virtue.

第一种译文说：符合天道，就要累积德性；第二种说：提前准备，就是累积德性。还有人把德性理解为精力。下面接着解释"积德"，"重积德，则无不克。"只要能够累积德性，尽其所能，发挥自己的最大力量，那就没有什么困难不能克服。译文也有两种：

1. With virtue accumulated, there is no difficulty but can be overcome.

2. With a good supply of virtue, one finds nothing impossible (all-conquering, nothing he is not fit for).

第一种译文实事求是；第二种说"征服一切""无所不适"，未免重了一点。下面又解释"无不克"，"无不克，则莫知其极。"没有不能克服的困难，就不知道力量到底有多大。译成英文则是：

With difficulty overcome, one's power knows no limit.

接着再解释"莫知其极"；"莫知其极，可以有国。"有了不知道多大的力量，那就可以治理国家了。因为，"有国之母，可以长久。"有了治国的根本原则，就是积德，积蓄力量来治理国家，那就要长治久安了。这两句话可以翻译如下：

With unlimited power of virtue, one can rule the state; ruled with accumulated virtue as basic principle, a state can long endure.

最后说道："是为深根固柢，长生久视之道。"也就是说，积德治国，

第五十九章 论积德

才是站得高,看得远,长治久安,根深蒂固的百年大计,英译就是:

Such is the deep-rooted, far-sighted principle of ruling an ever-lasting state.

第六十章

论德归

积德是方法,德归是目的。累积道德力量,使德归于自己,成了人的本性,这样治理国家,自然可以天下大治了。所以这一章说:"治大国若烹小鲜。"治理大国,就像烹调一样,像煎小鱼一样,不必翻来覆去,只要顺其自然,就可无为而治,举重若轻,使得国泰民安了,译成英文却有繁简两种:

    1. A large state should be ruled as a small fish is cooked.

    2. Ruling a large state resembles frying a small fish, it is inappropriate to turn it over frequently.

第一种译文简单,只说其然而不说所以然;第二种却解释了所以然。接下来没有讲如何治国,只是概括地说:按照"烹小鲜"之道治国的结果:"以道莅天下,其鬼不神。""道"主要是指"无为而治"之道;"其鬼不神"的解释却有不同,我们可以看看几种译文:

第六十章 论德归

1. If the world is ruled in conformity with the divine law, the spirits will lose their supernatural power (influence).

2. When the Tao prevails (is applied) in the world, even ghosts and spirits become harmless.

3. To govern the world with the Way, the apparitions will not function.

第一种译文说鬼神会失去超自然的神奇力量（或影响），第二种说会变得无害，第三种说会不起作用。三种译文都有道理，到底哪种更好？那还要看下文。下文接着说："非其鬼不神，其神不伤人。"说不是鬼不像神，而是神并不伤害人。既然说神不伤害人，那前面说"其鬼不神"就不应该是"无害"的意思，第二种译文就不如第一种；第三种说用"道"来治理国家，把"道"当作一种方法而不是一种原则，不太妥当。说鬼神不起作用，也不如说鬼不能起神奇的作用，更合原意。这句可以翻译如下：

It is not that they have lost their power, but that their power will do no harm.

说不是鬼神失去了神奇的力量，而是神奇的力量不会伤害人。这就说得通了。下面又接着说："非其神不伤人，圣人亦不伤人。"非但鬼神不伤人，圣人也不伤人。既然鬼神都不伤人，圣人是接近神的人，自然也不会伤害人了。这句话不难翻译：

Not only will their power do no harm, but the sage will not harm the people either.

于是结论是"夫两不相伤，故德交归焉。""两"字指谁？神和圣人或是圣人和人民？既然是"不相伤"，那就是圣人和人民了，所以又说

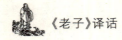《老子》译话

"德交归焉","交归"就是归于圣人和人民。结论可以英译如下:

  Since neither will harm the other, so virtue belongs to both.

第六十一章

论下流

上一章谈如何治理大国,这一章谈大国如何对待小国。"大国者下流,天下之交也。"如以高下而论,大国不应该高高在上,而应该处在低下的位置。因为天下的水都往低下的地方流,处在低下的位置上,就可以得到流水的好处。这句话有两种译文:

1. A large state should lie downstream in a low position where run all the streams.

2. Governing a large country is like lying in a lower place. This country in the world may be likened to rivers and streams flowing into the sea. It lies in a low position so that all in the world runs to it.

第一种译文基本是直译,第二种根据的版本不同,说得更加详细。这一句把"大小"比作"高低上下",下面一句比作"雌雄阴阳"说:"天下之交,牝常以静胜牡,以静为下。"天下男女交配,女方居下,男方居上,女方以静制动,胜过

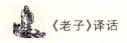《老子》译话

男方,译文只单一例:

> In the intercourse of the world the female call win the male by lying still in a low position.

"下"能胜"上","故大国以下小国,则取小国;小国以下大国,则取大国"。所以大国如果甘居下流,就可以赢得小国;小国如果甘居下游,也可以赢得大国。到了今天,"赢得"可以理解为得到信任,和平共处的意思。译成英文就是:

> So if a large state takes a low position, it may win over a small state. If a small state takes a low position, it may win a large state.

结果就是:"故或下以取,或下而取。"或者是处在低下的位置,以便取得小国的信任;或者是只要处在低下的位置上,就能得到大国的信任。译文也举两例:

1. So a low position may win or win over a state.
2. Some yield to win trust, others yield to be trusted.

第二种译文说:大国谦让可以得到信任,小国谦让,大国就信任了。下面接着具体说明:"大国不过欲兼畜人;小国不过欲入事人。"大国不过是要小国服从,小国不过是要大国保护而已。译成英文就是:

> A large state will only rule and protect and a small state will serve and be protected.

大国要统治,小国要保护,刚好相反相成。所以结论是:"夫两者各得其所欲,大者宜为下。"大国小国都能达到目的,所以大国应该尽

第六十一章　论下流

可能处在低下的位置。结论可以翻译如下：

Both states may attain their end, so a large state had better take a low position.

第六十二章

善与恶

　　国有大小,大国以下小国,可以蓄人;小国以下大国,可以事人。这就是说,大国平等对待小国,可以教育人民;小国得到平等对待,也可以为大国服务。所以说"大国者下流",就是说:平等对待大小国家,对双方都是有利的。平等之道不但可以应用于大国和小国,还可以应用到善人和恶人,所以第六十二章说:"道者万物之奥,善人之宝,不善人之所保。""奥"是奥妙,诀窍的意思,善人和不善人就是善与恶,好人和坏人。"宝"是动词,说善人把"道"当作宝贝一样重视,坏人却利用"道"来保护自己。例如"安全"之道就是一个例子,中国重视国家安全,领土完整,把这当作国家的核心利益;日本右倾军国主义分子占领了中国领土,拒不归还,反而借口"安全"来扩军备战,说是保卫自己,这就是"不善人之所保"了。这句译成英文有下列译法:

　　1. The divine law is the key to everything: the treasure for men of virtue and the protection for men

第六十二章 善与恶

without virtue.

2. The way (or Tao) is the shelter (refuge, storehouse, innermost recess) of all things; it is what the good men (kind people) cherish (keep, treasure) as well as what the bad men (unkind people) want to keep (preserve, protect).

比较一下几种译文,可能第一种比较好些。第二种的"道"译得不好理解,音译则叫人莫名其妙。"善恶"说成"好坏"虽然可以,但对道德的强调不如第一种。"奥"字的第二条内几种译法又太具体,反而不如抽象的好。

第六十二章接着说:"美言可以市尊;美行可以加人。"这就是说,说好话真诚动人,可以得到别人尊重敬爱;做了好事可以使人得到好处。这句话也可以有下列译法:

1. Fine words can win respect and fair deeds can influence people.

2. Beautiful (honored, flowery) words can buy (gain) respect (or are popular in social activities, can be sold like cheap trinkets), and beautiful (pretentious, fine) deeds can be highly regarded (can raise one man above others, can have an impact on others).

第一种译文简单明了,说好话可以赢得尊敬,做好事可以影响别人。第二条几种译文却更复杂,"美言"有的译成花言巧语,那就有贬义了,"市"字译成"买"也是一样;说"在社交活动中很流行"可能和原意有出入。"加人"如果说是"高度重视"或"使人高人一等",也都和原意不合,比较之下,可能还是第一种译文好一点。

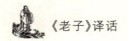《老子》译话

下面接着说:"不善之人,何弃之有?"这就是说,美言美行不只是对善人的,对不善的人也要说好话,做好事,不能抛弃他们,而要一视同仁。这是老子的重要思想,译文也有下列几种:

1. Even though without virtue, why should they be abandoned?

2. How can the bad man (the unkind people) desert (abandon) the Tao (the Way)?

第一种译文说:即使是不善的人也不应该抛弃,也要对他们说好话,做好事。第二种译文说不善的人怎么能抛弃"道",那就把不善的人从被动变成主动,上下文不相连接了,所以不如第一种译文好。

说好话,做好事,到了今天,一个国家说的好话就是理论建设,文化建设,做的好事主要是经济建设,政治建设,所以需要建立政府,任命官员。而在老子的时代,"故立天子,置三公、虽有拱璧,以先驷马,不如坐进此道"。这就是说,在封建时代,要由皇帝统治,任命公侯将相,他们虽然有金银珠宝,高车大马,但主要的还是进行治国之道。建设经济和文化。这几句话可以有下列译文:

1. Therefore the emperor is enthroned (ascends the throne) and the ministers (three ducal ministers) installed (appointed). Though they may have jadewares (jade disks) and chariots preceded by four steeds, it would be better to put the human law in practice.

2. On the occasion of a king's coronation or an official's inauguration, instead of receiving tributes of large jade and

第六十二章　善与恶

teams of horses, it is better to sit and receive the tribute of Tao (Way).

两种译文大同小异。第二种写的环境更具体,说在国王加冕或官员就职时,与其接受玉石马队的赠礼,不如用"道"作为献礼。但"道"作为献礼不好理解,不如第一种译文说理论付诸实践更加通俗易懂。第一种括弧中的"三公"已经过时,似乎不必直译。"道"字包括天道和人道,天道不能付诸实践,所以译成人道更好。

最后的结论是:"古之所以贵此道者何?不曰求之以得,有罪以免邪?故为天下贵。"这就是说:古人为什么把"道"的价值看得这么高呢?还不就是因为"求道"可以得道,有罪可以免罪吗?为什么老子说"有罪以免"呢?这是老子的重要思想,我想大约是因为"过而能改,善莫大焉。"有罪而能悔罪,改过自新,老子认为就可以免罪了。从正面讲,求道可以得道,从反面讲,有罪可以免罪,所以天下人都把"道"看得非常重要了。这个结论有几种译文:

1. Why should the ancients value the divine law? Is it not said that who seeks will find and who sins will be pardoned? That is why the law divine and human is valued in the world.

2. Why did ancients value the Tao so much? Was it not said that by making use of the Tao one could get what one desired or avoid punishment when committing an offense? That is why it is valued so much in the world.

3. Why did the ancients treasure this Tao? Wasn't it because followers of Tao get blessings for goodness and forgiveness for evil? Therefore, Tao is the greatest treasure

179

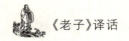

in the world.

三种译文各有千秋。第二、三种译文"道"字音译,不如第一种意译。"求之以得"第一种译文最泛,说是寻找就可以得到;第二种更具体。说是利用"道"就可以满足欲望;第三种更加具体,说是"道"的追随者做了好事可以得到福祉。"有罪以免"的三种译文也是一样:第一种的"罪"字译得最重,第二种译得更轻,说是"冒犯,得罪",第三种译文居中,说是做了错事可以得到宽恕。究竟哪种解释更好?那要联系实际来检验。例如第二次世界大战日本犯下了严重的侵略罪行,战后中国没有要求赔偿,这是不是"有罪以免"呢?我认为这要看日本是否悔过自新。根据日本军国主义分子否认侵略的罪行看来,和二战后的德国完全不同,它是不能"有罪以免"的。由此可见,运用老子思想也要具体情况具体分析。

第六十三章

难与易

《老子》第二章《辩证法》谈到美丑善恶的相对论,这一章却谈到难易大小也是相对的。但是这一章第一句是"为无为",那就是说,"为"和"无为"也是相对的了。关于"无为"第三章有专论,一开始说:"不尚贤,使民不争;不贵难得之货,使民不为盗;不见可欲,使民心不乱。"可见老子所说的"无为",并不是什么事都不做的意思。至少在第三章,他就举了三个"无为"的例子:一"不尚贤",二"不贵货",三"不欲"。用今天的话来说,"不尚贤"就是不提倡崇拜英雄贤人,为什么呢?"使民不争。"目的是使人不争取英雄贤臣的名位。反过来说,如果人不争名,那赞美贤德并不是不可以的。同样的道理,"不贵难得之货",就是不要看重难得的奇珍异宝,为什么呢?"使民不为盗。"因为贪图难得之货,就会造成腐败堕落的官僚,甚至杀人放火的强盗。由此可见"不尚贤""不贵货"就是反对争名夺利。"不见可欲"更是从根本上说:不要贪心。如不贪心,自然不会有争名夺利的欲望,那就是"民心不

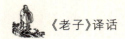

乱",人人安分守己了。这样看来,本章第一句"为无为"并不是什么事也不要做,而是不要争名夺利,只要安分守己的意思。如果这样理解,那么"为无为"就不能译成 do nothing,而应该加词译为:

  Do nothing wrong.

同样的道理,接下来的"事无事"就应该是:做事不要自私自利,而要做利人利己的事;"味无味"也应该是:饮食不要贪图山珍海味,能够充饥解渴就是美味了。如果这样理解,那这三句可以简单译成:

  Do nothing wrong, selfish or greedy!

但是下文接着说:"大小多少,图难于其易,为大于其细,天下难事,必作于易;天下大事,必作于细。"可见老子是把"为"与"无为"和大小、多少、难易几对矛盾联系起来谈的。既然困难的大事必须从容易的细小部分做起,那"事无事"又可以理解为"把大事当作小事一样来做";"味无味"却可以理解为"把粗茶淡饭当作山珍海味一样来吃"。那这三句的译文又可以是:

  Do nothing wrong. Do a deed as if it were not a deed. Take the tasteless as if it were tasteful.

有的译本把"为无为"翻译如下:

  1. Act by means of inaction.
  2. Act without taking visible action.

第一种译文的意思似乎是:用不行动的方法来行动,是否词能达意呢?这就要读者来回答了。第二种译文说:行动要采取看不见的行动方式。是不是会引起误解,以为老子主张隐秘行动呢?

第六十三章　难与易

这也是个仁者见仁,智者见智的问题。但是根据老子接着说的"大小多少"看来,可能还是前面的译文合理一些,好懂一些。老子的意思是:事情无论大小难易,困难的大事也有比较容易的部分。所以做困难的大事要从比较容易的部分做起。这段话可以翻译如下:

> Big or small, any difficulty has more or less easy parts, any great deed has small details. There is nothing difficult but consists of easy parts; there is no great deed but consists of small details.

但是这段话有不同的理解,如北京大学出版社译本就理解为:大以小为基础,多以少为基础。克服困难,要从容易的部分做起;完成大事,要从小事做起。用英文说就是:

> The big stems from the small; the many is based on the few.
>
> To overcome the difficult should begin with the easy;
>
> To accomplish what is big should begin with the small.

这译文的好处是提出了"克服困难"和"完成大事"两个动词,如果补充第一种译文的"难易"关系:

> There is nothing difficult but consists of easy parts.

上下文的联系可能更好一点。

外文出版社的文本不同:"天下之难事,必作于易;天下之大事,必作于细。图难于其易也,为大于其细也。"译文也不相同:

> It is a rule in the world that the most difficult things

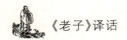

begin with the easy, and the largest things arise from the minute. Hence, tackle the difficult while it is still easy; achieve the large while it is still minute.

译文说:天下难事开始是容易的,大事起于小事。因此,当难事还容易做的时候,就要动手;当大事还小的时候,就要去做。这个译文和原文不同,难事开始容易,大事起于小事,都不是老子的话,也不符合老子思想,这里就不讨论了。

这段话的结论是:"是以圣人终不为大,故能成其大。"因为圣贤知道"天下大事必作于细",所以他做大事一定从小事做起,最后才能做成大事。这个结论和"大事起于小事"不同,可以翻译如下:

Therefore the sage never tries to be great at first, but he becomes great at last.

北京大学出版社的译文是:

That is why the sage can accomplish what is great by never attempting to be great.

译文还原可以是:圣人从来没有打算成为伟人,所以才能做成大事。中文把伟人和人事分开了,英文却是同一个字两个意思,这就有矛盾了,所以第二种译文不如第一种好。辽宁大学出版社的译文是:

The sage never attempts to do great deeds; in this way, he completely succeeds.

译文还原可以是:圣人从不打算做大事,这样他就完全成功了。原文"从不为大"并不是说"从不打算做大事";"完全成功了"会使人

第六十三章 难与易

误以为完全没有做成大事,和原意完全相反。"大事必作于细"原意是大事必须在小处下工夫,一点一滴不放过。这是关于"大小"的结论。

关于"难易"的结论,老子先从反面说起:"夫轻诺必寡信,多易必多难。是以圣人犹难之,故终无难矣。"这就是说:轻易许诺必定失信,低估困难必定碰到困难更多。聪明人事先想到各种困难,结果做起事来反而不难了。这就是"难易"的辩证关系,可以翻译如下:

> A rash promise will soon be broken; much underestimation will entail much difficulty; therefore, the sage anticipates all difficulties: so there is nothing difficult in the end.

总而言之,本章的结论是:难事必作于易,大事必作于细。

第六十四章

成与败

上一章谈难易,结论是:难事必作于易。怎样化难为易呢?这一章接着谈:"其安易持,"意思是说:安稳的状态容易保持;"其未兆易谋。"坏事还没有露出苗头,就容易扼杀在摇篮里。"其脆易泮,"脆弱的东西容易打碎;"其微易散。"微小的东西容易失散。了解了事物的性质就容易办了。所以结论是:"为之于未有,治之于未乱。"这就是说:凡事要有先见之明,不等乱子发生,就先消灭得无影无踪。这一段可以译成英文如下:

> It is easy to hold what is stable, to plan before trouble should rise, to break what is fragile, to disperse what is small. Make preparations before things happen; keep order before disorder sets in.

第一段谈的是抽象理论,第二段接着谈具体事例。"合抱之木生于毫末,"要几个人围起来才抱得拢的大树,开始生长的时候也只是小小的根芽;"九层之台起于累土,"九层高的楼台开始建筑的时候也只是几个土堆;"千

第六十四章 成与败

里之行始于足下，"一千里的长途也是一步一步走完的。这就是说，困难的事开始并不困难，而是一点一滴累积而成的。这样解释就化难为易了。第二段可以英译如下：

> A huge tree grows out of a small shoot; a nine-storied tower rises from a heap of earth; a thousand-mile journey begins with the first step.

第一段是"起"，第二段是"承"，第三段就"转"了。如果不能一步一步化难为易呢？那么就会"为者败之，执者失之。"结果却会是欲速则不达，贪得反失之。"足以圣人无为故无败，无执故无失。""无为"是老子的重要思想，但并不是什么都不做的意思。根据上下文来看，这里"无为"是"不急于求成"，而要一步一步化难为易，否则就会失败，即使得到，如果是固执地自私自利，那也会失掉的。这一段可以考虑翻译如下：

> Who is too eager for success will fail, too eager for gain will lose. Therefore, the sage is not too eager in doing anything for himself, nor does he hold any gain too tight for himself.

最后一段是"合"："民之从事常于几成而败之。"这就是说：人们急于求成，往往快成功了，最后还是失败，所以第一个结论是："慎终如始，则无败事。"最后要像最初一样，一步一步化难为易，那就不会失败。第二个结论是："是以圣人欲不欲，不贵难得之货，学不学。"也就是说，聪明人没有自私自利的欲望，不贪图奇珍异货，也不学习自私自利。学什么呢？最后的结论是："复众人之所过，以辅万物之自然，而不敢为。"这就是说：要弥补别人的错误，不妨

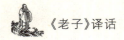《老子》译话

碍万物自然状态,这样才能成功,不致失败。可以考虑如下英译:

People engaged in a task often fail on the brink of success. If cautious from the beginning to the end, he would not have failed. Therefore, the sage desires to be desireless or selfless, he never values what is hard to get, he learns to be unlearned for himself. He tries to mend the fault of others and to help all things develop naturally without his interference.

第六十五章

智 与 愚

这一章谈到"以智治国"和愚民政策的问题,引起的争论不少。在我看来,这是一个对"智"与"愚"的理解问题。老子在这里所说的"智",是指钩心斗角,尔虞我诈;所说的"愚",是指回归自然,返朴归真的意思。如果这样理解,就可以豁然贯通了。

本章一开始说:"古之善为道者,非以明民,将以愚之。"这就是说:古代懂得治国之道的人,并不是要使人变得聪明诡诈,强词夺理,而是要使人热爱自然,天真淳朴。所以不能按照字面,把"明民"理解为使人聪明,把"愚之"理解为愚民。这句可以译成英文如下:

> The ancients who followed the divine law would not use sophism or sophisticate the public mind but simplify it.

关于"愚"字,我见到的几个译本郁用 simple 或 simplify,只有一本用了 keep the dark(在黑暗中),那就有愚昧无知的意思了。

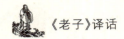《老子》译话

下面接着说:"民之难治,以其智多。故以智治国,国之贼;不以智治国,国之福。"老子的意思是:如果一个国家的领导人用花言巧语欺骗人民,使人民上当受害,那就是一个国贼。例如第二次世界大战时的日本军国主义者,把侵略亚洲国家说成是"建设东亚共荣圈",欺骗日本人民当兵,到国外去杀人抢劫,结果不少日本人也送了命。而这些日本军国主义者就是大大的国贼。现在日本的右翼领导人还在参拜靖国神社中的二战战犯,用花言巧语来欺骗日本人民,要重新扩军备战,这些领导人就是新的国贼。和日本形成鲜明对照的是德国。二战后的德国领导人承认战时犯下的罪行,并且坚决改正,不再重犯,这样不再用花言巧语来欺骗人民,才能使人民过上和平幸福的生活。老子的这段话可以译成如下的英文:

The people would be unruly because sophism is (was) used. To rule the state by sophism is to do harm to it; to rule it on the contrary is to do it good.

上面一段比较了"以智治国"和"不以智治国",接着说:"知此两者亦稽式。""稽式"就指两种治国方式。"常知稽式,是谓玄德。"知道了两种治国方式的优劣,那就是明白了天道,有的注解说:天道就是玄德。因此可以说:老子认为不以智治国是符合天道的。"玄德深矣,远矣,与物反矣,然后乃至大顺。"玄德既然是指天道,那天道自然是深奥的、悠久的,万物都要按照天道发展,最后返归自然,人也一样,无论智者愚者,国也一样,无论以智治国还是不以智治国,结果都要按照天道发展,最后回归自然。这段理解不够深刻,勉强译成英文如下,仅供参考。

第六十五章 智与愚

In the rule by sophism and by unsophism we see two types of government. If we know the types, we can by and by know the mysterious divine law. The mysterious law is profound and far-reaching. In the end everything will return to nature in accordance with the divine law.

这一章理解不深刻,因为各人理解不同,有人认为老子的"弃智"和"愚民"是无政府主义的学说,我认为古人的学说要古为今用,要设想古人在今天的情况下会怎样说,我就怎样理解了。

第六十六章

论不争

  治国以智或不以智,这是一个路线问题。不与人争上下先后,这是一个道德问题。老子说:"江海所以能为百谷王者,以其能下之,故能为百谷王。"江和海所以能容纳百川,容纳百谷之水,因为江海都处在低下的位置,所以可引领百川之水,似乎成了山谷之水的领导。这句话有两种译文:

  1. The sea can lord it over all the streams flowing from hundreds of vales, for it takes a lower position, so water flows into it from hundreds of vales.

  2. All the streamlets flow towards the river and the sea because the latter takes the lower position. Hence the latter becomes the king of countless valleys.

  第一种译文说:江海能够君临千百谷地流来的河水,因为江海位置更低,所以河水就流入江海了。第二种译文大

第六十六章　论不争

同小异,说江海成了谷地的君王。老子先举实例,然后上升为理论说:"是以(圣人)欲上民,必以言下之;欲先民,必以身后之。"所以领导人如要身居百姓之上,那言语必须谦虚谨慎;如要领导群众,那一定不能与民争利,争先恐后,译文如下:

1. If you want to be higher than the people, you must learn to be humble in words; if you want to go before them, you must learn to stay behind in person.

2. If the sage is to guide the people, he must speak in modest terms; if the sage is to lead the people, he must follow behind.

两种译文大致相同,第二种用词(除"圣人"和"民"外)更加简明。结果会怎样呢?"是以圣人处上,而民不重;处前,而民不害。"所以领导人虽然在百姓之上,百姓在下面并不感觉到有压力;领导即使处在领先地位,群众也不觉得有什么妨害。这句可有几种译文:

1. So when the sage is high above, the people do not feel his weight; when he is at their head, they feel no harm.

2. Thus the sage, though being placed high over the people, never burdens the people; the sage, though going ahead of the people, never stands in the way of the people.

3. Therefore, the sage leads without doing harm, and guides without being oppressive.

第一种译文基本直译;第二种重复"圣人"和"人民"太多,似乎没有必要,但"害"字译得明确;第三种译文更简明,"不重"和"不害"颠倒了次序。最后的结论是:"是以天下乐推而不厌。以其不争,故天

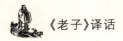《老子》译话

下莫能与之争。"所以天下人乐于推崇他,而不感到厌烦。他不和人争斗(争名夺利),天下人也就无法和他争了。"不争"是老子的重要思想,是个人修养之道,但是不是治国之道就需要研究了。结论可以翻译如下:

> That is why the world praises him without getting tired. As he will not contend, so none in the world can contend with him.

第六十七章

慈之道

"天下皆谓我道大",全世界都说"道"大,例如《礼记》就说:"大道之行也,天下为公。""大道"就是天下为公之道。天下为公,不是为私,还有比这更大的道理么?天下为公,公也包括私在内,因为公私是矛盾统一的。当公利和私利统一的时候,公利既利人又利己,公私两利;但当公利和私利有矛盾的时候,那就不能损公肥私,而要公而忘私,这就是天下为公,说"我道大"的原因。下面接着说:"似不肖"。"不肖"是什么意思?一种说法是:道大得没有什么可以相比。另一种说法是:道是大而抽象的,不像任何具体的东西。我觉得第一种说法好一些。下文又接着说:"夫唯大,故似不肖;若肖,久矣其细也夫。"这就是说,正因为道大,所以没有什么可以相比;如果有什么可以相比,那大道也成了细枝末节,不成其为大道了。这一段可以译成英文如下:

All the world knows that the divine law is great and there is nothing like it. Since it is great, so nothing can be like it. If there is anything like it, it would not have been so great.

第二段说："我有三宝，持而保之：一曰慈，二曰俭，三曰不敢为天下先。"老子要行大道，有三件宝贝拿在手里经常使用。既然说是可以拿在手里的宝贝，那就不能说不像具体的东西，所以上面第二种说法不如第一种。不过老子说的"三宝"倒都是抽象的：第一宝是对人要慈爱，第二宝是用物要节俭，第三宝是做事不要勇于争名夺位。译成英文可以如下：

> I have three treasures which I hold and keep: the first is magnanimity (kindness, mercy, compassion) the second frugality (thrift, restraint) and the third humility or to be the last of the world (unwillingness to take the lead, to be ahead,...)

第一宝是老子"爱的哲学"，第三宝是"不争哲学"。不争名利很好，如果工作也不争先，那就是消极因素，不合时代要求了。下面接着谈三宝的好处："慈故能勇，俭故能广，不敢为天下先故能成器长。"慈爱才能勇敢，节俭才能宽厚，不争名位才能领导。这段可以翻译如下：

> The magnanimous can be courageous, the frugal can be generous, the humble last can be the leader of the world.

第一段"起"，第二段"承"，第三段"转"："今舍慈且勇，舍俭且广，舍后且先，死矣。"意思是说：勇敢而不仁慈就会乱杀无辜，慷慨而不节俭就会浪费财物，争先就会没有后盾，结果都非失败不可。译成英文就是：

第六十七章 慈之道

Courage without magnanimity, generosity without frugality, the front without the rear are doomed to failure.

第四段是"合",主要谈第一宝。"夫慈以战则胜,以守则固。天将救之,以慈卫之。"结论是说:勇敢而又仁慈符合天道,可以得到上天保佑,对于仁慈的战士,上天也是仁慈的。结论可翻译如下:

The magnanimous will be victorious in war and steadfast in defense. Heaven would favor them and protect them with magnanimity.

第六十八章

智仁勇

第六十五章谈"智","以智治国"不能钩心斗角,营私舞弊,所以要"仁"。第六十七章说:"慈故能勇","慈"就是仁慈,内心仁慈,外表才能勇敢,勇于助人,不是害人。这是智、仁、勇三者的关系。

上一章谈到"慈以战则胜",说勇敢而仁慈的人在战争中才能取得胜利。这一章接着说:"善为士者不武","士"指知识分子,也有人说是指领导,那就是说:领导战争的人不要诉诸武力,而要以智取胜。"善战者不怒",即使在战争中,也不要一怒之下就逞匹夫之勇,而是要有仁心,有勇有谋。"善胜敌者不与",有的书解释说:"不与"就是不与敌人战斗,而用智谋,甚至是用仁德去取得胜利。这几句有几种译法:

1. A good (wise) warrior is not violent, a good (skillful) fighter is not angry, a good fighter (clever winner) may win without fighting (is not vengeful), a good (masterful) leader will be humble (is not

第六十八章 智仁勇

pretentious).

2. An adept commander did not display his martial prowess. An adept warrior did not become angry. An adept conqueror did not tussle with his enemy. An adept manager of men placed himself below them.

3. He who is good at being a commander does not display his bravery; he who is good at fighting does not burst into anger; he who is good at defeating his enemy does not brace himself to engage in a tough battle; he who is good at employing men humbles himself before them.

4. Those who are good at commanding do not resort to force; those who are good at fighting are not easily irrigated; those who are good at subjugating the enemies do not fight battles with them; those who are good at using people are modest towards them.

几种译法繁简不同，用词有相似有不似，但基本上大同小异，这里就不一一讨论了。最后总结说："是谓不争之德,是谓用人之力,是谓配天古之极。"这就是说，"不武""不怒""不与"都是"不争"之德，也是"用人"之才。这样德才兼备，就既合乎人道，也合乎天道了。译文可有下列几种：

1. Such is the virtue of non-contention (non-competition), the ability of employing men (use of others' force). Such is the way (supreme principle) to match heaven.

2. This is the virtue of avoiding competition; this is the art of dealing with people. This is the way of conforming

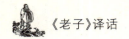

to Tao.

3. This is called the virtue of non-contention; this is called making use of others's trength; this is called conformability to the Tao of heaven.

4. This is called the quality of not vying with others; this is called the ability to use people; this is in agreement with the Way of Heaven.

第六十九章

攻与守

上一章谈到战争与不争的问题,这一章进一步谈战争的主客攻守。一开始说:"用兵有言:吾不敢为主而为客,不敢进寸而退尺。"用兵的军事家说:"我不愿意主动进攻敌人,只愿意打被动的保卫战。我宁愿守军退后十步,也不愿意侵略的军队前进一步。"这说出了老子的反战思想,其实代表了中国自古以来反对侵略战争、热爱和平的理论,驳斥了日本右倾军国主义分子污蔑中国"威胁"好战的无耻谎言。这句话可以译成下列英文:

1. A strategist said, "I will not take the offensive but the defensive; I will not advance an inch but retreat a foot."

2. A strategist says: I dare not launch an attack but strengthen defense capabilities (Take the defensive rather than the offensive); I dare not advance an inch but retreat a foot instead (give a foot rather than take an inch).

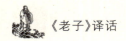《老子》译话

以上两种译文，第一种简洁明了，第二种比较冗长，比较一下括弧中的第三种译文就可以看出，第三种和第一种大同小异。

第一段是"起"，第二段是"承"："是谓行无行，攘无臂，执无兵，扔无敌。"这就是说：行军而不进军，举起手臂而不打击，拿起武器是为锻炼而不是打仗，舞刀弄枪不是面对敌人。第一段谈整体比较抽象，第二段谈个体比较形象化。这一段有下列译文：

1. This means marching without advancing, raising arms without striking, holding when there is no weapon and striking when there is no enemy.

2. This is known as marching without revealing your ranks, rolling up your sleeves without showing your arms and carrying weapons without disclosing them—such is the way to be ever victorious.

第一种译文还是简明，第二种更形象化：说进军而不暴露队伍，卷起袖子而不露出胳臂，带了武器却不让人看见，相当巧妙。但是原文版本不同，最后四字是"乃无敌矣"，所以译成这是永远胜利的方法。

第三段一"转"说："祸莫大于轻敌，轻敌几丧吾宝。"老子虽然反对战争，但当敌人把战争强加于人的时候，却宁可把敌人看得强大一点，不可小看对方，否则，战争失败，就要失掉宝贵的和平生活了。这段可以翻译如下：

1. No danger is greater than making light of the foe, which may lead to the loss of our treasure (peaceful life).

2. No disaster is more serious than underestimating the

第六十九章 攻与守

enemy; it results in the loss of one's three treasures.

第二种译文比较具体,"宝"字译成前面提到的"慈俭"等三宝。但说战争使人失去"慈俭",不如说失掉和平生活更加合理。

最后两句的结论说:"故抗兵相加,哀者胜矣。"这就是说,如果对抗双方力量相差不大,那么受侵略的一方会取得最后的胜利。这几乎总结了中国的抗日战争史。结论可以译为:

When two fighting forces are equal in strength, the wronged side will win victory.

第七十章

内与外

老子说:"吾言甚易知,甚易行;天下莫能知,莫能行。"老子说的话很容易理解,也很容易实行;但是却没有人懂得,也没有人做到。为什么呢?老子回答说:"言有宗,事有君。"因为他说的话都有根据,他做的事都有道理。根据什么?根据天道。例如上一章说的:"哀者胜矣",一般人理解的却是"强者胜矣",所以做的事就是侵略扩张;不知道强弱是相对的,是可以转化的:得道多助,失道寡助。例如第二次世界大战时,日本恃强侵略中国,中国抗战合乎天道,得到盟国协助,最后打败日本,就是说明"哀者胜矣"的一个例子。这一段话可有下列译文:

1. It is very easy to understand what I say and put it into practice, but it is not understood and not put into practice in the world. My words reveal the divine law and my deeds reveal the human law.

2. My words are very easy to understand and very easy to put into practice, yet there should have

第七十章　内与外

been no one in the world who can understand them and can put them into practice. Words must be purpose-oriented, deeds must be reasonably grounded.

第二种译文最后说：说话总有目的，做事总有合理的根据，而第一种说的却是：说话根据天道，做事根据人道。两者理解不同，但都各自言之成理。

老子接着说："夫唯无知，是以不我知。知我者希，则我贵矣。"这就是说，因为不懂天道，所以也不懂我的话。物以稀为贵，懂我的人越少，我说的话就更加可贵了。这几句话可以翻译如下：

1. People who do not know my words (the divine law), so they do not understand me. Few people understand me, so I am all the more valuable.

2. Because the people are ignorant, they do not understand me; they make me all the more honored.

"无知"的译文第二种比第一种重，"贵"的译文又比第一种轻。何去何从，读者可以自己选择。

最后老子说："是以圣人被褐而怀玉。"这是用具体的例子来说明无知的人重外表而轻内心，聪明人却重内心而轻外表，所以外面穿着粗布衣服，内心却很丰富，有用之不尽、取之不竭的金玉珠宝。译成英文可有下列三种：

1. That is why the sage wears plain clothes but his heart is pure as jade.

2. That is why the sage is always dressed in coarse cloth but conceals about him a beautiful piece of jade (the Tao).

205

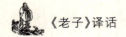《老子》译话

3. Thus, the sage's outer appearance belies his inner worth.

比较三种译文,可以说第一种简明,第二种用词更具体,第三种最抽象,只说外表内心不同,真是各有千秋。

第七十一章

认识论

在这一章中,老子又谈到他的认识论。一开始说:"知不知上,不知知病。"这就是说,知道自己不知道,就说不知道,这是上策;分明不知道,却以为自己知道,这就是毛病,是错误了。这两句等于说:知之为知之,不知为不知,是知也。译成英文可有几种方法:

1. It is good to know that you do not know; it is wrong to pretend to know what you do not.

2. Knowing one's ignorance is strength; ignoring one's ignorance is weakness.

3. It is your merit if you know your own ignorance; it is your demerit if you do not know, but appear to know it.

三种译文把"上"和"病"分别译成对错,强弱,优点和缺点,各有千秋。后两种把"不知"说成"无知"似乎太重。

老子接着说:"夫唯病病,是以不病。"知道自己错了,就不会再犯错误了。译文可以是:

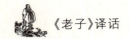《老子》译话

1. Since you know what is wrong, you will not be wrong.

但有两种译文把这两句和下一句"圣人不病"合译如下:

2. The sage is of no shortcoming, because he considers shortcoming as shortcoming.

3. The sage has no weakness because he knows weakness as weakness.

上两句的"病病"和"不病"是通称,圣人"不病"是特称。似和原意不合。所以第一种译文把"圣人不病"和下文"以其病病,是以不病"合译如下:

1. The sage is not wrong, for he knows what is wrong, so he will do no wrong.

老子的认识论在第一章中就说到了:"道可道,非常道。"就是说:道理是可以知道的,但不一定是你所知道的道理。这里又进一步分析为两种态度:一种是知道什么是错误,所以不犯错误;另一种是不知道,所以错误就会重犯。

自第六十二章到第七十一章是后来补写的,写法和其他各章大同小异,如有重复,就要请原谅了。补完《〈老子〉译话》之后,可以小结一下,觉得《老子》给自己印象最深的,还是"无为""不争"。但我理解的"无为",根据老子的相对论看来,应该是"无为而无不为"。"无为"是指不做任何不符合"道"的事、或违反自然的事、或干涉别人自由的事;"无不为"却是相反:只要是符合"道"或自然规律的事,就没有不可以做的,只要是别人按照"道"发挥个人自由,就不应该干涉,不但不该干涉,而且要让别人充分发挥自由,这才是"无不为"。至于"不争",应该分"收入"和"付出":不应该争收

第七十一章 认识论

入,如个人名利;但应该争付出,如付出劳动,做出成就。九十多年来,我前三十年是"争名夺利"时期;中间三十年是"少为""少争"时期;50年代我不能自由译著,只出版了四本中英法文互译作品,80年代以后三十多年是"无不为而不争"时期,领导"无为",让我自由发挥,结果出版中英法文著译120余本,成了全世界有史以来"诗译英法唯一人",这也是"无为而无不为"的一个例子。

第七十二章

论不厌

上一章主要谈自知,这一章进一步谈知人的问题。"民不畏威,则大威至。"领导人不但要有自知之明,还要了解被领导的民众。如果人民群众不怕领导人滥用权威,那就说明他们有更大的力量。对于"威"的理解可能不同,我们先来看看译文:

1. If the people fear no power, it shows that theirs is greater.

2. When the people are not afraid of the threatening might of the authority, the great tumult will soon ensue.

3. If people are not fearful of your authority, disorder will arise.

4. When people do not fear the power of the ruler, something terribly dreadful will take place.

5. When the people stand in no fear of the intimidation of the rulers, there will be greater impending disasters.

第七十二章 论不厌

比较一下五种译文,可以看出除了第一种译文用同一个词译"威"字之外,其他四种都用了两个不同的词。第一种用了 power(权力,力量),表示人民不怕强权,因为他们的力量更大。第二种用了 might(强权)和 tumult(混乱),说如果人民不怕当权者的恐吓,那表示大混乱就要发生了。这个说法比第一种更严重得多。第三种用的词是 authority(权威)和 disorder(不安),不如第二种译文严重,和第一种差不多。第四种用了 power 和 something terribly dreadful(可怕的事情),前半和第三种差不多,后半比"不安"更严重,第五种也说"恐吓"(intimidation)和"灾难"(disaster),严重的程度接近第二种译文。由此可见五种译文大同小异,只是轻重程度不同,译者可以见仁见智,根据老子"无为""不争"的思想看来,程度轻点的译文可能更好,为了避免发生混乱,老子接着说:"无狎其所居,无厌其所生,夫惟不厌,是以不厌。"不要扰乱人民群众居住的地方,不要干扰他们的生活,统治者不扰乱人民群众,老百姓也就不会扰乱社会了。这几句可以翻译如下:

> Do not deprive them of their houses (harass their living places), nor interfere in their life (deprive them of their means of livelihood). If you do not interfere in their life (oppress the people), they will not make trouble in social life (be tired of you).

最后的结论是:"是以圣人自知不自见,自爱不自责,故去彼取此。"所以领导不能干扰人民,要有自知之明,不能表现自己有所作为而干扰别人。要尊重自己也尊重别人,不能自以为是,而要表里如一,对人如同对己,不分彼此。这个结论也可以翻译如下:

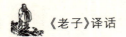《老子》译话

Therefore the sage knows himself but does not show off; he respects but not overvalue himself. It would be better to know and respect oneself than to overvalue oneself and show off.

第七十三章

论争胜

上一章谈到不表现自我,不重视自己,轻视别人,总而言之,就是不争,不争强好胜,这一章更进一步,说明可以不争而胜,先从反面说起:"勇于敢则杀,勇于不敢则活。""勇"和"敢"有什么不同?一般说来,"敢"指胆大。"不敢"指小心。这就是说,胆大粗心的人容易招惹杀身之祸,胆大心细的人却可以延年益寿。我们再看几种不同的译文是怎样说的:

1. Brave and daring, one will be killed; brave and not daring, one will survive.

2. Bravery in being bold leads to death; bravery in being timid leads to life.

3. He who dares to risk will perish; he who dares to yield will survive.

4. If you are bold enough to be strong, you are doomed; if you are bold enough to be weak, you are saved.

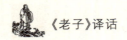《老子》译话

第一种译文把勇敢和粗心大胆分开;第二种说勇敢大胆会走向死亡,勇敢胆小却能生存。"胆小"似乎不如"心细"。第三种说敢冒险者死,敢顺从者生,似乎是在鼓励投降主义,这和原意不合。第四种说勇敢逞强者注定灭亡,勇于示弱者可以得救。"示弱"超过了"不敢"。看来还是第一种译文稳妥些。下面接着说:"此两者,或利或害,天之所恶,孰知其故?是以圣人犹难之。"两者指"敢"与"不敢",敢之有害,不敢者有利,谁知道上天为什么喜欢哪一个呢?连圣人都为难啊,这话可以译成英文如下:

> Which of the two will do good or harm? Who knows the reason why Heaven hates one or the other? It is even difficult for the sage to understand.

上面的话是个问句,其实答案已经有了,所以下面就说:"天之道,不争而善胜,不言而善应,不召而自来,默然而善谋。"天道(或自然规律)就是不必争夺,却能胜利;不必说话,却已应对;不必召唤,却已自动来了,外表沉默寡言,内心却是多谋略,善规划,不争而胜是这一章的重点,可以翻译如下:

> In accordance with Heaven's divine law, one may win without contending (fighting), respond without speaking, come without summons and plan well without discussion.

最后的结论是:"天网恢恢,疏而不漏。"宋代范应元注说:"恢,大也,包罗无外,如大网焉,虽稀疏而不失巨细,善恶皆不可逃也。"这就是说:天道(自然规律)像一张大网,善恶都有报应,可以翻译如下:

> Heaven spreads a boundless net and none could escape from its sparse meshes.

第七十四章

论畏死

关于生死问题,上一章谈到"勇于敢"则死,"勇于不敢"则生,举了四种译文为例。结合这一章的"民不畏死,奈何以死惧之?"看来,"敢"和"畏"是相反的对立面,说人民不怕死,用死来吓唬人什么用?所以"勇于敢则杀,勇于不敢则活"的意思应该是:一个勇敢的人如果只是敢做这事,敢做那事,结果不是杀身成仁,就是身败名裂;如果他虽然勇敢,却不敢犯任何错误,那才能够功成身退,符合无为不争的思想,所以这句应该翻译如下:

> Bravery in daring would lead to death (A brave man who dare do wrong will fail); but bravery in not daring would lead to life (a brave man who dare not make mistakes will succeed).

而"民不畏死,奈何以死惧之?"就是说老百姓是"勇于不敢"的,如果他们不敢犯法,用"勇于敢"的办法来恐吓他们,怎能吓倒人呢?这句可以译成英文如下:

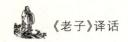《老子》译话

The people do not fear death. Why threaten them with it?

接着又从正反两个方面来说:"若使民常畏死,而为奇者,吾得执而杀之,孰敢?"宋代苏辙说:"民安于政,长乐生畏死,然后执其诡异乱群者而杀之、孰敢不服哉?"如果国泰民安,百姓乐生畏死,而有犯法作乱的人,那就可以处以死刑。那么,谁还敢犯法作乱呢?译成英文可以有几种:

If they (the people) ever fear it (death), those who do evil (go against law, make trouble) will be caught (arrested) and killed, who then would do evil again (be offenders, trouble-makers)?

但是谁来执法?谁来判处死刑?下文回答说:"常有司杀者杀。"那就是说:有管理司法的人来执行死刑。接着又对司法人员做了限制;"夫代司杀者杀,是谓代大匠斫,希有不伤其手者矣。"如果不是司法人员,却要来代替法官执行死刑,那就像鲁班门前弄大斧一样,要代替木匠作木工,哪能不砍伤自己的手呢?下面看看几种译文:

1. It is the executioner's duty to kill. If you replace him (if one wants to kill on behalf of the executioner), it is like cutting wood in a carpenter's place, how can you not wound your hand? (few can escape cutting their own hands.)

2. Executioners will still be needed. Unwise rulers are like would-be carpenters; if they are eager to try their hand, then few will escape without hurting their hands.

3. There is always a master in charge of execution. To

第七十四章　论畏死

carry out executions in place of the master is like hewing wood in place of a skilful carpenter. Very few escape cutting their own hands.

# 第七十五章

论生死

这一章继续谈生死问题,但是先从饥饿谈起。"民之饥,以其上食税之多,是以饥。"老百姓所以饥饿,因为统治者收税太多,百姓上税太多,自己就吃不饱,甚至饥饿而死,这话可有几种译文:

1. The people's starvation (hunger) results from the rulers' over-taxation (exorbitant taxes), so the people starve (are hungry).

2. The people suffer from famine because the ruler levies too much tax-grain (the rulers are guilty of overtaxation). Thus they suffer from famine (That is why the people feel starved).

"饥"字译成 starvation(饿死)比 hunger(饥饿)重,比 famine(灾荒)轻,"税"字译成 overtaxation(税收过重)则又不如 exorbitant taxation(过分超越正轨的税收)重。因为苛捐杂税太重,百姓难以为生,所以下面接着说:"民之难治,以其上之有为,是以难治。"老百姓不容易管理,因

第七十五章 论生死

为统治者的所作所为有所不当,收税太重,所以国家就不好治理了,译文也有以下几种:

> The people are difficult to rule (unruly, rebellious), for the rulers give exacting orders (interfere too much, too often take action, meddlesome actions), so the people are hard to rule (to control).

"难治"译成 difficult to rule(难于治理)不错,如用 to control(控制)则更强调统治者一面,如用 unruly(不守规矩)的则有谴责老百姓的意思,如用 rebellious(反抗的,叛乱的)那就更严重了,不过今天的反抗精神倒有积极的一面。下面的"有为"译成 too often take action(过分经常采取行动)没有说明行动正确与否,是否符合老子思想可以研究,我看不如说 meddlesome action(多管闲事的行动)更加明确,如用 exacting orders(苛刻的命令)则对统治者有贬义,可能还是用不褒不贬的 interfere too much(干涉太多)更好,下面又由治乱转到生死问题:"民之轻死,以其上求生之厚,是以轻死。"说老百姓不重视生死问题,因为统治者太看重自己的生命。太看轻别人的生死存亡,所以百姓也不在乎生死了,译成英文就是:

> The people make light of their death (do not take death seriously), for the rulers overvalue their own life (lead a luxuriant and dissipated life), so the people undervalue their death.

"轻死"的译文,括弧中从反面说;"厚生"的译文,括弧中却加重说是骄奢淫逸的生活,和前译文大同小异,最后的结论是:"夫唯无以生为者,是贤于贵生。""无以生为"就是生而无为,不把生命看得太

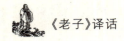《老子》译话

重,"贵生"却是把生命看得太贵重,重不如轻,译文如下:

> Those who have no use of life (make light of life) are better (wiser) than those who value (overvalue) their life.

括弧中的译文都更明确,所以比直译好。

第七十六章

论强弱

上一章谈到生死和治乱的轻重关系,这一章谈生死和强弱刚柔的问题。"人之生也柔弱,其死也坚强。"一般人认为生者是强者,死者是弱者。老子却从另外一个角度来看,说生命是脆弱的、柔弱、死亡反倒是强硬的、刚强的,因为人活着的时候,身体是柔软的,死后反而变僵硬了,这话译成英文可有下列几种:

1. Man is born soft and weak; dead, he becomes hard and stiff.

2. While alive, a man's body is supple (soft and tender); when dead, it becomes hard (and stiff).

第一种译文更对称,但"弱"的反面是"强",英文没有译成 strong(强大,坚强),却译为 stiff(坚硬,僵硬),因为英文可以说:死亡是强者,若说死者是强者,就可能造成误解了。第二种译文用词更具体,但不如第一种对称,两种译文各有长短。下面从人的生死,说到万物的生死;"草木之生也柔脆,其死也枯槁。"说草木生长的时候也是柔软

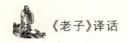

的、脆弱的,但枯死的时候,也就形同槁木死灰了。译文英文就是:

  Grass and trees grow soft and supple(fragile); dead, they become dry and withered.

于是结论就是:"故坚强者死之徒,柔弱者生之徒。"这样看来,坚硬是死亡的特性,柔软是生存的特点。译成英文可有几种方法:

  So the hard and strong belong to death (are the companions of death, are of the dying sort), while the soft and weak belong to life(are companions of life, are of the living sort).

几种译文大同小异,说坚强属于死亡,是死亡的伴侣,是死一类的;而柔弱属于生命,是生命的伴侣,是生一类的。这个结论是否正确,可以研究,因为如果说强者会死亡,弱者能生存,难道弱者不会死亡,强者不能生存么?也都是有生有死的,不过总起来说,强者人数较少,生存时间较短;弱者人数较多,总的生存时间更长而已。下面又把强弱问题扩大到军事方面说:"是以兵强则灭,木强则折。"这个推论也有问题,难道兵弱不灭,木弱不折么?恰恰相反,兵弱可能灭得更快,木弱应该折得更早。所以这话的意思只是物极必反,兵强总要灭亡,木强总会折断而已。译成英文就是:

  Therefore, a strong army will be annihilated(shattered, destroyed, wiped out, may fail in its attacks); a sturdy tree will be cut down(broken, felled down, is ready for the axe).

第七十六章 论强弱

译文轻重略有不同,可以不必讨论,最后的结论是:"坚强处下,柔弱处上。"坚强占了下风,柔弱占了上风,结论可以翻译如下:

The soft and weak may have the upper hand of the hard and strong.

第七十七章

论高下

上一章谈到强弱的高下,结论与众不同,说是弱者高于强者,因为强者易折易灭,反而不如弱者长久。这一章继续谈高下问题:"天之道,其犹张弓欤?高者抑之,下者举之。"老子把天道比作弯弓射箭之道;弓举高了,要压低点;压得太低,又要举高一点,结果既不能太高,也不能太低,而要不高不低,一箭射中目标。这种张弓射箭的,是符合自然之道的。下面看看几种英译文:

1. Is riot the divine law like the art of bending a bow? When the bow aims too high, it should be bent down; when it aims too low, it should be lifted up.

2. Is the law of nature (the Tao or Dao of heaven or Heaven) not just like the drawing (bending, aiming or stretching) of the bow? When the string is too high (taut, overstretched), it is lowered (pressed down, loosened); when it is too low (understretched), it is raised (lifted up, tightened).

第七十七章 论高下

第一种译文用了动词 aim（瞄准），可以达意；其他译文多是译词，意思不够清楚，下面又从高下谈到有余和不足："有余者损之，不足者补之。天之道，损有余而补不足。"这样就把有余比作高，把不足比作下，天道既是抑高举低，自然要抑富济贫了。译文就是：

1. We take form those who have enough and to spare and give to those who have not enough. In accordance with the divine law, excess should be reduced to supplement the insufficient.

2. It is the law of nature to reduce what is abundant (excessive) and replenish (compensate) what is lacking (deficient).

在两种译文中，第一种用词比第二种更平易，下面接着又从天道谈到人道："人之道则不然，损不足以奉有余。孰能有余以奉天下？唯有道者。"人间的道理似乎和天道不同，却使贫者愈贫，富者愈富，贫富分化，越来越严重。什么人能按照天道行事，使天下穷人都富起来呢？那就只有得道的人。老子的"道"到底是平均主义，还是社会主义的先声？可以研究，这几句可译成英文如下：

The human law is different; man takes from the poor to give to the rick. Who could give to the poor world more than enough? Only the follower of the divine law.

最后的结论是："是以圣人为而不恃，功成而不处，其不欲见贤。"所以领导人做了事只是尽了本分，没有什么了不起，不能居功自傲，甚至不应该认为自己做了什么好事，是个贤人。结论的译文是：

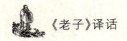《老子》译话

So the sage gives without being the giver, and succeeds without being the successful (claiming for credit), for he will not be better than others (show off his wisdom).

第七十八章

论刚柔

第七十六章谈了生死和强弱刚柔的关系,这一章继续刚柔和治国的问题。"天下莫柔弱于水,而攻坚强者莫之能胜,其无以易之。"老子认为天下最柔弱的是水,但是水滴石穿,柔弱的却可以战胜强硬的,而坚硬的并不能代替软弱的。这话的译文有下列几种:

1. Nothing in the world is softer and weaker (more supple) than water, but nothing is better (more powerful) to win over (in attacking) the hard and the strong, for it cannot be replaced (because nothing can take its place).

2. In this world there is nothing softer than water, which has seen no rival (nothing surpasses it, no force can compare with it) in wearing away hard things, because there is no substitute for it (nothing is its equal).

几种译文大同小异,第一种的"刚柔弱强"译得比第二种

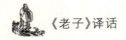
《老子》译话

更对称,第二种的"攻"字译成 wearing away 很好,更能体现"水滴石穿"之意,下面接着说:"弱之胜强,柔之胜刚,天下莫不知,莫能行。"弱者能够胜过强者,柔软的能够胜过坚硬,这是天下人都知道的,但却不是天下都做得到的。这话译成现代汉语,加了"能够"二字,表示只是有可能性;又说"不是都做得到的",从反面来说可以看出老子的话应该与时俱进,到了今天还可应用,这话可以翻译如下:

> The weak may surpass (overcomes, is more powerful or stronger than) the strong and the soft may surpass (overcomes, is more rigid or harder than) the hard, it is wellknown to the world, but none can put it into practice.
> (括弧中的动词不如用 may 好)

几种译文差别不大,说 stronger than the strong 和 harder than the hard 重复;"强硬"二字是好是坏,意见可能不同。最后把刚柔强弱应用到国家的统治者身上说:"是以圣人云:'受国之垢,是谓社稷主;受国不祥,是为天下王。'正言若反。"所以圣人说:"领导人如果能够为国家忍辱负重,那就可以做社会的主人;如果能够经受苦难的考验,那就可以做世界上的帝王。"这话听起来似乎不太对,像是反面说法,其实是正确的道理。结论有如下几种大同小异的英译文:

> That is the reason why the sage says,"Who can bear the contempt (disgrace, humiliation) of (on behalf of) a state may become (be called, is worthy to be called) its master (priest, sovereign); who can endure the diaster of a state

228

第七十八章 论刚柔

(shoulder the responsibility for the calamity of the state) may become its ruler." It seems wrong, but it is right. (Factual words seem ironical. Such truthful words often sound paradoxical. Positive words seem to be their opposite).

第七十九章

论德怨

上一章谈到"弱之胜强",这一章谈以德报怨的问题。"和大怨必有余怨,报怨以德,安可以为善?"人和人之间如果有深仇大恨,能不能调和呢?即使能够,会不会有余恨难消?如果以德报怨,是不是更好一点?我们看看几种译文:

  1. Implacable hatred cannot be wholly appeased. Would it not be better to return good for evil?(不可调和的仇恨不能完全消解,那么以德报怨会不会好一点呢?)

  2. When the great enmity is allayed, there must be some remaining hostility; even if one requites hostility with kindness, how could that be considered perfect?(深仇大恨即使减轻了,一定还有剩余的敌意;即使用好意来回报敌意,难道能算是完善的办法?)

第七十九章　论德怨

3. When a bitter hatred is resolved, some resentment lingers; how is this satisfying? （仇恨解决了，余恨还不消散，怎能令人满意?）

4. To reconcile two sides in deep hatred is surely to leave some hatred behind. If one returns good for evil, how can this be taken as a proper solution? （要调解有深刻仇恨的双方，一定会留下余恨。如果以德报怨，那能算是正当的解决办法呢?）

5. To mediate the deepest enmity, there will still be enmity left after the mediation; can it be called the right way to solve problems if the Virtue is repaid with enmity? （要做两个冤家对头的中间人，调解后总还会有敌意存在，以怨报德，能够算是解决问题的正道吗?）

五种译文五花齐放，各有千秋，都说以德报怨不是解决深仇大恨的办法，第一种译文态度温和，只是提出问题；第三种原文删了"以德报怨"几个字，第五种译文改成"以怨报德"了，到底应该如何解决问题呢? 老子下面答道："是以圣人执左契，而不责于人。""左契"是借债的欠条。这就是说，圣人只拿着欠条，并不要求借债人还钱，既不以德报怨，也不怨怨相报，借债人还也好，不还也好，只是任其自然。这就是老子的"无为"之道，译成英文就是：

So the sage keeps the receipt, but never demands its payment.

最后的结论是："有德司契，无德司彻。天道无亲，常与善人。"有德的人只是放债，保持欠条，并不放弃债务，也不要求还债，一切

231

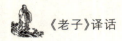《老子》译话

任其自然,自己只是"无为"。至于"无德司彻",几种译文的理解都是:没有道德的人则苛刻要求彻底还债。但是天道一视同仁,不分亲疏,既然善人按照天道做事,所以天道常在善人一边。这个结论可以英译如下:

> A man of virtue keeps the receipt; a man without virtue exacts the payment. The divine law is impartial, but it favors the good men (or men of virtue).

第八十章

论小国

上一章说:"有德司契,无德司彻。"从形式上看,是说有道德的人只管借钱给别人,没有道德的人却只要求彻底还债。从内容上看,却是有德的领导人只管给予,无德的统治者只是索取。讲的是老子的政治原则。这一章讲的是老子的政治理想:"小国寡民,使有什佰之器,而不用。"国家要小,人民要少,使用的器具虽然是人口的十倍,甚至百倍,人民却没有那么多的用处。老子的时代人口多了,国家大了,所以争执多了,战争爆发了,老子认为不如恢复到静心寡欲的古代,国家小了,可以"无为"而治;人少器多,可以"不争"而生。这个政治理想有以下两种英译文:

1. A small state with few people may have hundreds of tools but will not use them (have no use of them).

2. The state should be small, but the population should be sparse. Tools, though of many kinds, should not be used.

《老子》译话

第一种译文是叙事,不如第二种谈理想。但第二种后来说器具不应该用,又不如第一种说"用不着"。下面继续用实例来谈理想:"使民重死而不远徙。虽有舟舆无所乘之;虽有甲兵无所陈之;使人复结绳而用之。"理想的国家使人民看重生命,不肯轻易死亡,也不肯迁居去远方;虽然有车有船,却不肯用来远游;虽然有武器有盔甲,也不肯用来打仗;甚至宁愿恢复到结绳记事的远古时代。这种复古的思想今天看来落后得可笑,但却反映了古代人对战争发生的恐惧。这些理想的实例可以译成英文如下:

> Its people value their life and death(Teach the people to fear death)and will not remove far away; they may have boats and cars, but they have no need to ride; they may have armours and weapons, but they have no need to use them; they may return to the age of recording by tying knots(Encourage them to return).

第一种译文还是叙事。括弧中的译文用命令语气,教育人民不要怕死,鼓励他们回到结绳记事的古代。两种译文可以取长补短合而为一。最后的结论是:"至治之极,甘其食,美其服,安其居,乐其俗。邻国扣望,鸡犬之声相闻,民至老死不相往来。"到了统治的最高(理想)境界,人民都吃得好,穿得好,住得好,生活快乐,听得见邻国的鸡鸣狗吠,但是一生都没有来往。译成英文就是:

> In an ideal state the people will find their food delicious, their clothes beautiful, their houses comfortable, their life delightful. A neighboring state may be within sight, with cocks' crow and dogs' bark within hearing, but people (of the two states) will not visit each other till they die of old age.

第八十一章

论信美

《老子》的最后一章开始谈美学,最后谈"为而不争"的哲学,可以说是老子思想的总结。一开始说:"信言不美,美言不信。"认为,值得相信的老实话往往并不好听,听得并不顺耳,而好听的话往往又不可信,说的是内容和形式的矛盾。形式好看的,内容不一定可信,内容可信的,形式又不一定好看。要求内容和形式两全其美,实在是不容易。这个矛盾可以译成英文如下:

> Truthful words may not be beautiful; beautiful words may not be truthful.

这个矛盾应用到文学翻译上来,就是求真(忠实性)与求美(艺术性)的矛盾,英国有个诗人曾开玩笑把翻译比作妻子说:

> A faithful wife is not beautiful; a beautiful wife is not faithful. (忠实的妻子往往不美丽;美丽的妻子往往不忠实。)

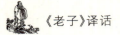《老子》译话

所以文学翻译就成了"不忠实的妻子"。不过一般说来,文学作品都是艺术性而不是科学性的,如果译文只求真而不求美,严格说来,并不能算是忠实于原文,所以文学翻译应该是既求真又求美的。而真和美的矛盾起源于老子,所以可以算是老子的美学思想。接着,老子把信和美的矛盾扩展到"善"和"知"的方面来说:"善者不辩,辩者不善。知者不博,博者不知。"好人并不说自己好,说自己好反而不好;聪明人不一定知识广博,知识广博的人也不一定聪明。译成英文就是:

> A good man need not justify himself; who justifies himself may not be a good man. A learned man may not be wise; a wise man may not be learned.

上面说的是善者和知者对自己的态度。至于如何对待别人呢?老子接着说:"圣人不积,既以为人己愈有,既以与人己愈多。"这是老子的重要思想;圣人不累积任何东西,任何东西都用来帮助别人,别人的东西也都成了自己的,所以帮助别人越多,自己拥有的也越多;给予别人的东西越多,自己保存的东西也越多。用英文说就是:

> A sage does not keep things for himself. The more he helps others, the more he still has. The more he gives, the more he keeps.

最后的结论是:"天之道,利而不害;圣人之道,为而不争。"天道是顺其自然,人和万物都是顺自然发展,天道自然对他们都有利无害,圣人之道是"为而不争"。前面刚刚讲了:"既以为人"是用来帮助别人的意思,所以"为"就是"助人","与人"就是"给予","不争"应该是不争名利,但是要争"助人",要争"给予",这才是圣人之

第八十一章　论信美

道。结论可以翻译如下:

> The divine law will do all good and no harm. They way of a sage is to help and to give but not to strive to take.

最后这两句话是老子《道德经》的总结。"天之道,利而不害"这是对"道"的小结。总而言之,"道"对人和万物是有利无害的,怎见得?如果不是有利,人和万物就不可能生长发展到现在的情况,这是用结果来说明原因。第二句话说:"圣人之道,为而不争。"这是对"德"的小结,因为"道"是客观规律,是不依人的思想转移的,而"德"是社会规律,是可以随人的思想而改变的,圣人之道就是顺应天道,顺其自然,做对人和万物有利的事,这就是圣人之"德"。"德"是"为而不争","为"是做好事,这也说明了老子的"无为"不是不做事,而是不做坏事,不干涉别人做好事的意思,"不争"却是不争名夺利,这是从反面来讲"德"。前面说了,《老子》第三十七章以前讲"道",以后讲"德",这是从正反两面来讲对"德"的认识。以前怎么讲"德"?多半是从反面讲的。如第三十八章说:"上德不德",说有"德"的人并不认为自己有"德",这种"认为"本身就是"德","德"就是"得",人和万物看到没顺应自然,所得到的就是"德",或德性。第三十九章说:"万物得一以生。"万物顺应天道,就得到了自己的本性或德性,就能生长发展。第四十九章说:"善者吾善之,不善者吾亦善之,德善。"这就是说,老百姓对我好,我也对他们好;即使对我不好的人,我对他们也一样好,这样,老百姓就都好起来了,大家都得到了好的德性。这就是老子以德报怨的思想,也是他治国的德性。关于治国,第五十七章说:"以正治国,以奇用兵。"治国要用正道。什么是正道呢?"我无为,而民自化。"这就是无为而治,不做错事,不做对人有害无利的事,不妨碍人发展,而能以身作则,人民自然会顺其自然,发挥主观能动性,做有利无害的事。第六十五章说:"以智治国,国之贼;以不智治国,国之福。"这里的"智",指的是阴谋诡计,歪门邪道的智谋,所以对国家有害,不能给国家带来福利。至于用兵,第六十九章说:"用兵有言;吾不敢为主而为客。"用兵不应该主动进攻侵略,而只能够被动防御守卫。最后又说:"哀者胜矣。"侵略军会失败,被侵略的哀军会取得最后的胜利。无为而治,以身作则是治国者的"德",防御守卫是用兵者的"德"。总的说来,"德"是"为而不争",顺应天道自然,做对国家人民有利的事,不争个人的利益,这就是"德"。

《道德经》的下篇除了"德"外,也谈到道和德的关系,谈得更多的是辩证关系:贵贱,高下,正反,有无,刚柔,进退,虚实,巧拙,成败,盈虚,曲直,知行,损益,生死,祸福,宽严,善恶,难易,先后,强弱等等。最后的结论是第八十一章说的:"既以为人己愈有,既以与人己愈多。"如果无私,为人做事就是为自己做事,给予别人等于给予自己,所以给得越多,得到的也越多,这就是多少有无的辩证关系。总之,老子的思想可以概括为:无为而治的政治理想,与世无争的经济思想,无私知足的人生哲学。